Polpop 2

Polpop 2
Politics and Popular
Culture in America Today

James Combs

Bowling Green State University Popular Press
Bowling Green, Ohio 43403

Dedication

In memory of
Harold Doak Young

Contents

Preface

This is the second edition of a book first published in 1984. The Presidency of Ronald Reagan has come and gone, and the United States has gone to war again. The national government has been firmly in the grip of established elites with a very uncertain political mandate, leading to very unclear policies and results. If Machiavelli were alive today to revise his great treatise, he might write of us as not in the age of the lion or the fox but of the weasel. The politics of the 1980s and 1990s includes a great deal of ambivalence, stemming at least in part from the rapidly changing position of the United States in the world. That political ambivalence included the elite attitude toward popular culture. No less a personage as the head of the National Endowment for the Humanities decried the study of popular culture as less than worthwhile. Yet she served two Presidents who used popular culture to advantage at every turn, who also headed a government that hoped to influence and even suppress aspects of popular culture they did not find politically advantageous. Such recognition of the power of popular culture might then justify its study. The fulminations of NEH appointees and suchlike should inspire us all the more to examine the politics of popular culture. In that spirit, I decided the time was ripe to look at politics and popular culture today.

Thanks are due to Carol Lewis, who patiently and efficiently guided the manuscript into readable form. The support of the Political Science Department and Vice-President for Academic Affairs at Valparaiso University was indispensable. Bowling Green, as always, was helpful and prompt. Much recent work in the Popular Culture Association and the "Popular Communication" section of the International Communication Association has been helpful. And, as always, heartfelt thanks to Sara, the last best wife.

James Combs

1

Chapter One
Popular Culture and American Politics

This book is a study of the relationship between popular culture and politics. It is done in the conviction that there is an important and consequential interrelationship between popular culture and politics. The many forms of popular culture with which we are all familiar—popular music, movies, television, books, and so on— are part of our learning experience, and thus help to shape our imagination about the world. Even though much popular culture seems at first glance "non-political," this does not mean that it has nothing to do with politics. And even though what we usually think of as "politics"—the comings and goings of Presidents, the deliberations of Congress, decisions by the Supreme Court—also seems on face to have little to do with popular culture, on reflection we can discover relationships that are significant if subtle. For politics occurs in the context of our popular experience, and in that sense is not immune from the flow of popular discourse. In the United States, and in many other countries, when we speak of "popular politics," we are recognizing that politics has a popular component, and is affected by the many forms of experience of the populace. Too, we recognize that popular culture is affected by the ebb and flow of political tides, and that indeed the creations of popular culture are a major way of understanding the attitudes and images that underlie conservation and change in politics. Both our popular and political experience are linked by imagination, and if we can understand cultural imagination, we have gone a long way toward penetrating the mystery of culture.

Culture

There is a character in a play by Moliere who was astonished and pleased to learn that he had been speaking prose all of his life. It also might interest the reader of this book to learn that she or he has been speaking poetry all of their lives too. In other

2

words, all of us learn how to use the various "languages of communication" available to us. From birth, our education proceeds by acquiring the ability to communicate, and the capacity to use that communication in order to cope. We learn to speak various languages of prose—administrative, technical, educational—for purposes of dealing with bureaucracies, computers, and schoolteachers. But prose tends to be prosaic—functional, rational, and goal-oriented. But humans are also poets, and learn to speak in poetry. We learn that we do not live by bread alone, but through languages of communication that are poetic. We all acquire a sense that the world we live in means something, and that such a poetic meaning is something that can be communicated and shared. When we see a sunset, or go through a death in the family, or fall in love, we move into the realm of poetic language that more adequately captures the depth and tone of our experience.

When we say that "we are all poets," this suggests that we all learn, and use, an *aesthetic sensibility*. In our daily lives, we go about the mundane habits and situations that are our common fare. In school, at work, filling out a form, dealing with a car repairman—all such activities are largely dealt with in the language of prose. But our aesthetic sense gives us the idea that life is more than prose. So we add poetry, or what is termed "symbolic meaning" to life, and by so doing, imbue it with language that attributes to it our sense of aesthetics. Thus an aesthetic sensibility is simply a poetic way of knowing, feeling, and acting toward the world as we understand and share it. This can range from the crudest to the most sophisticated evaluations of beauty, and ugliness, good and bad, fair or foul, harmonious or discordant, the exhilarating and the depressing. Our aesthetic sense impels us not only to characterize experience, but also to evaluate it. When we do something in everyday life, we may not attach a great deal of importance to it, and it remains part of our prosaic world. Habits such as brushing our teeth, and workaday activities such as processing data become second nature which invite little reflection. But if we do something to which we attach symbolic meaning, then we have added poetry to it. If we make work into the symbol "work" with meaning surrounding it, then it has taken on aesthetic significance for our life. "Work" is part of "career," one of the major projects of our life; the "work ethic" becomes part of what we believe in; "working" part of what everyone else worth anything should do; "reward" something that we justly deserve as compensation for a job well done; and "consumption" something that we do to reward ourselves with pleasurable goods and services. Taken separately, all these activities might remain prosaic and unreflected upon; but when they are related together as part of our "reflexive consciousness," they then become poetry, acquiring the complex of symbolic meanings that give our lives aesthetic significance. As the word "symbol" suggests, taken together, these activities stand for something, experience transformed into imaginative narrative of which we are the central character. In other words, imaginative narrative about ourselves and what our life means becomes the basis for autobiography, and all other forms of storytelling. Our aesthetic sensibility transforms life into *story*— our story, other's stories, traditions of stories, kinds of stories, canons of stories, metastories (stories about stories).

A great, and almost universal, human tendency is, then, to turn individual experience into a narrative that can be communicated to self and others. Not only do we make sense out of our own past lives by telling stories about them, we make sense of our future lives. We reconstruct the past, making sense of memory, often altering and justifying the past, and indeed, even wishing that we had done some things differently (what you might call "retrohearsing"). We project the future, rehearsing what might happen and what we wish would happen, but in any case ordering experience that has not yet occurred into a story as if it had already happened. By so doing, we anticipate the future through the power of imagination. But we are not alone. We learn a good bit of what our own lives are supposed to be from other people. "Significant others" tell us stories they have learned from people before them, and we tell stories to young people—our children, for example— who come after us. Most stories are not idiosyncratic, but rather are a part of *culture*.

A cultural story is a shared and perpetuated narrative that instructs, entertains, and in some cases represents important symbolic meanings of particular culture values. Such stories may range from fairy tales to complex epic poems, but in all instances they are shared by a population that holds their value in common, and wishes to see them perpetuated over time. Children's stories divert and delight the audience to whom they are told, but they usually also have a didactic purpose: they tell kids who they are, who we are as a group, and what it is that they should value and expect to be and do. Further, some stories are taken to be so important as to be representative of the culture as a whole. In the United States, we tell children stories about individual achievement ("The Little Engine That Could") as opposed to the Russians, who tell Soviet children stories about group adjustment and cooperation. We retell stories about individual heroism that saves the good people and their values from external evil, beginning with the Western but moved now into city streets and outer space. Such tales are representations of democratic heroism that we should value and admire, in, say, a President or a policeperson. At least in part, cultures are perpetuated (and changed) by stories, tales that place in the context of time and circumstance a sense of identity put in aesthetic symbols. We learn to identify ourselves and our world through the stories that we are told, complemented with the stories that we tell ourselves based on our own experience and imagination. For a good part of our learning occurs in *play.*

When we see children at play, we are observing a setting in which the children are using the occasion to "play at society." They are learning what has been called "sociation," the ways to properly communicate with other social beings. They learn cultural mores and folkways, both formal and informal ways of thinking and acting. It is more than battles that are won on playing-fields; our very conceptions of self, role, and social order are given impetus by what we discover in playing. In a broader sense, play is the social context of the development of our aesthetic sensibility. The poetry of life is learned through play. In school, you learned how to read through learning the alphabet, the meaning of words, how to construct sentences, how to read and speak and write. But when the grade school teacher read your class a story, then the play of your imagination was aroused, and you were learning all about adventure and achievement, the virtues of conflict and cooperation, the relationship between men and women, how to recognize heroes, villains, and fools, and what to expect as to the outcome of stories. Such storytelling teaches us *cultural aesthetics*, representing through symbolic play the poetry of our existence as a people. Play may be imaginary, but it is not random, nor is it inconsequential. The relationship between the "play world" and the "real world," between fantasy and reality, imagination and action, story and actuality is tenuous and reciprocal, but nevertheless has an enormous impact on what we expect, hope and fear the world out there will be like.

Our education in cultural aesthetics teaches us the lessons of the playforms of societies, usually ordered as *drama*. When we render the world understandable as aesthetic experience, we are imagining it as it is given symbolic order in the various forms of theater. When children play "house," they are engaging in a "'tend like" play-form of society as drama, performing their roles in a proto-family that at the moment has only aesthetic existence in the shared experience of the play. In play, life is theater, an aesthetic experience given immediate symbolic meaning in a dramatic format that serves as a kind of anticipatory rehearsal for subsequent action in social roles such as "spouse." Even when we play alone, in make-believe or daydreaming, we place ourselves in a social drama in which we hope to control the conduct of the action and the outcome of the story, and wish that we could make real life live up to the expectations that we develop in dramatic imaginings. In any case, our aesthetic sensibility gives us an ability to understand, and act in, social dramas, giving us histrionic resources (lines, gestures, etc.) and more importantly an idea of what cultural dramas we come across are significant and how they are supposed to come out. Such ideas, we must stress again, are not private and idiosyncratic musings unshared across a population. "Culture," after all, is both subjective and objective, something people inherit, use, and pass on, and something public, expressed, and negotiated over time. In the modern world, culture is not confined to elite or folk enclaves, but has rather become the province of the populace at large.[1]

Popular Culture

Just as with speaking prose daily, we usually do not reflect on the fact that we are all carriers of culture. Nor are we much aware of the particular historical and social conditions that make most of us the carriers of something called "popular culture." In its broadest aspect, popular culture is the culture of the populace. But in itself, that is not something new: the populace in traditional pre-modern societies or folk enclaves had a culture, including folklore, music, dance, rituals, indeed a vast ensemble of popular expressions codified into habitual and ongoing culture. But popular culture as we experience it is a modern phenomenon, the explosive product of "the great transformation" of the last few centuries that created modernity. The inclusive and expanding social, economic, and political movements of that period of time have brought modern history to its present condition, including now one of its most momentous creations, popular culture. What we experience as popular culture stems from our cultural imagination, but it is given popular expression largely through the modern media of communication in response to how we have imagined the creations and thrust of modernity. Popular culture may be a universal social fact, but it is in its modern form an immediate experience. However, we may delimit and define popular culture, its major historical usage has been to help us understand and respond to the world in which we live now. Popular culture in this sense is the aesthetic expression of the modern condition represented in the various modes of popular communication developed during that period. The endless flood of popular books, magazines, newspapers, radio and television programs, movies, musical recordings, indeed all forms of expression widely consumed by a populace have both aesthetic and pragmatic functions. Such creations give us aesthetic treatments of what's happening as the dialectic of popular creators and audiences come to conceive them; and more subtly, and pragmatically, audiences find in them instruction as well as diversion, cues as to how to cope with life in the present. This is not to say that popular culture is cut off from the past or future; quite the contrary, our aesthetic and pragmatic use of it in the present links the past and future to the present. The Western and *Star Trek* are about our past and future, respectively, but they are both very much about our present.

Think, for example, of dolls. Children play with dolls, whiling away free hours in what appears to be harmless and superficial diversion. But nothing could be further from the case. Think of what psychologist Erik Erikson wrote: "Child's play is the infantile form of the human ability to deal with experience by creating model situations and to master reality by experiment and planning."[2] Children growing up in the late twentieth century play with dolls for fun, but it is not idle play. For in that play they are learning about contemporary sex roles, heroic action, proper relationships, what society values, and how to dress for work or play, love or war. A large measure of such learning is what we might call "implicit culture" because it is suggestive play-learning that is "caught, not taught," ideas and images picked up from the flow of popular discourse.[3] Consider a little girl playing with a Barbie doll. What might she learn from Barbie? What does Barbie "tell" her about norms of female beauty, what roles women can and cannot play, how they should relate to men, and what sort of values are implicit in Barbie's "lifestyle"? Barbie is a popular doll (estimates are that over 500 million of them have been sold to date, not to mention the many accessories, including designer clothes, and her friends, such as boyfriend Ken), and clearly a cultural artifact with widespread sanction among the populace. The child playing with her places her in imaginary "model situations," stories that develop conceptions of self in action because the child identifies with Barbie, and can imagine herself in the future in situations—stories about self—that she learned were desirable in her play with Barbie. In her present as a young child, Barbie is a means of diversion but also "anticipatory socialization," giving the child an aesthetic sense of the poetry of social action she can begin to emulate by "dressing up" and "looking nice" now in the presence of significant others. Later, as a young woman, Barbie has set a cultural standard for her, a standard of lithe beauty and high consumption that may be beyond her reach, but also a standard of female independence and choice that makes for dissatisfaction with "traditional" home-maker-and-mother roles. However, Barbie does not age nor gain weight, so as an important cultural icon she may contribute to female anxieties about aging or fat (*anorexia nervosa* is a familiar pathological reaction to that widespread fear). To adjust, adult women seek other "role models" who do cope with aging and bodily depreciation in later periods of their life, more appropriate and helpful than the unattainable and eternally youthful Barbie. Similarly, young boys who play with "G.I. Joe" dolls may learn aggressive attitudes and love of the military, which might not subsequently serve them well in civilian adulthood.

It is the underlying thesis of this book, and much of the literature on popular culture in general, that the power and influence of popular culture has increased mightily during the twentieth century. We have alluded to many of the reasons for this already—the development of modern culture, the advent of the mass media, the creation of prosperity and leisure time. What such a sweeping vision of recent history gives us is the idea that contemporary popular culture is no accident, but rather is the outcome of some identifiable processes that lead to say, children playing with, and learning from, popular toys. We not only must envision popular culture as rooted in our existential tendencies, but also our historical condition. It helps to think of *popular culture as an historical movement,* the consequence of forces that made modern people and modern things. Barbie, and all that she stands for, is no less the outcome of recent history than consumer capitalism and democratic institutions, and popular culture as a force is no less consequential.

Although it is second nature to most of us, popular culture as we understand and use it is something relatively new in the world. Indeed, another underlying thesis that informs this and many other books on popular culture is *the popularization of the world,* the recent historical development of the validity and indeed the supremacy of popular choice and popular will in matters of culture, economics, and politics. In other words, popular culture as a movement was swept into our world by the tides of democracy and capitalism, both of which include in their ideological justification a kind of "popular principle": ultimate power rightly resides in what the populace chooses. The social foundation of popular culture developed from the premise of political democracy that the people rule, and that public opinion and popular sentiment have a power that is difficult to resist. (Recall the apocryphal local candidate for offices who explained to a crowd of voters his stands on the issues, and then concluded hopefully, "Those are my views, folks, and if you don't like them, I'll change them.") Too, capitalism includes a popular principle in the assertion that if people want to buy something, it is their right and also the right of capitalists to produce it for them. In the marketplace as well as the voting booth, popular choice is supreme and fickle, and the eternal gamble of both politicians and investors is what ideas or products to bet on. This is not to say, of course, that the people doing the political or economic "selling" do not have a great deal of influence over the "buyers," through persuasion and manipulation. But it is to say that in the modern world people act upon this popular principle as if it were true and they were making free choices about who to vote for and what to buy. Although the constraints on those choices are many, the principle is truly popular in that the impulse toward "rising demands and expectations" as in democratic participation (as in South Africa and China) and consumer economics (Eastern Europe) is a widespread, and difficult to control, modern tendency. Given the logical premises of the popular ideology that has informed political and economic modernity, we should expect that culture would experience the same process of popularization. Although in some sense much past culture (such as the Greek and Elizabethan playwrights) was more popular than the guardians of "high culture" were willing to admit, it was with modernity that we may witness cultural popularization. Children have always played with dolls, but it took the conditions and resources of modernity to create, market, and value Barbie.

This view of modernity suggests the idea that once a powerful ideology and system of action grips large populations and States, it involves a "logic" that expands as a force over time in both power and application. The historical and social course of modernity has been given impetus and direction by the logic of democracy and the logic of capitalism. Over a long period of time, the historical force and sociological themes inherent in such a movement work out their logic, diffusing innovations, institutionalizing charisma, and establishing habits of thought and action. With the establishment of popular principles in economy, polity, and culture, we are observing the *logic of a popular order*. In such a world, we should logically expect the exercise of powers and choices that tend a popular order (albeit with considerable resistance from moral, taste, or elite cultures) towards manifestations of popular "political logic" (populist politics), economic logic ("expressive" and conspicuous consumption), and "socio-logic" (popular culture). When we study popular culture, we must take into account the historical context and interrelated social habits and institutions that make for the "logic" of popular activities. We do not reflect much on the logic of popular activity, but when we are concerned about our "popularity" with a peer group, or buy something because it is fashionable and "in" at the moment, or watch a TV show because "everyone else is," we are implicitly acknowledging the power of popular logic on our choice of activities. In a larger sense, we are participating in the furtherance of a popular order by our actions, "voting" with our ballots, dollars, and interests for those things that have popular appeal. In this way, the "popularity principle" becomes part of the essential logic of a popular order, affecting the conduct of politics, the emphasis of the economy, and the nature of culture.

The idea that modern societies are characterized by the dynamic unfolding of a "popular logic" was perhaps first analyzed in detail by Tocqueville. He toured the United States during the Age of Jackson, and began to observe social webs of meaning from which he could draw valid inferences as to the trends and direction of a democratic society. He found the emerging common culture of Americans a major source of *popular evidence*, in those activities from which we may infer something important about the logic of a society. Tocqueville inferred something important about American society from such sources of evidence as the evolution of a single word ("gentleman"), children's games and the etiquette of a public dance, and a music hall pageant in honor of Andrew Jackson. He often used the familiar metaphor of society as an interwoven and incomplete tapestry, a fabric raveled (and unraveled) over time by the inherent logic of the culture.[4]

In a popular order such as the United States, it is the raveling of *popular discourse* that offers us evidence as to the nature and direction of such a society. A social fabric is comprised of meanings defined in present situations, and since multiple meanings may emerge, a social order at a given moment may resemble a crazy quilt. But even though the raveling of the social tapestry may occur in a present, it is interwoven with the sometimes tattered fabric of the past and with the anticipated warp and woof of the future. In the present of the late twentieth century, it is our thesis that popular culture in America and increasingly around the world has become a potent and explosive social force. For more and more people, popular culture may have become a primary rather than secondary source of learning. If that is becoming the case, then it becomes the task of inquiry to examine popular discourse for evidence of the imaginative basis of continuity and change as it is interwoven into the social tapestry.

Political Culture

It is our specific task to interweave two major aspects of American culture, the popular and the political. We are looking for the ways in which these aspects of culture affect each other. Political culture includes all those distinctive ways of political thinking, feeling, and doing that make one country identifiably different from another. But in a popular order, political culture is not confined to elite habits and institutions. A popular society is also characterized by popular politics, the exercise of power in a popular setting that features both the imaginative and participatory presence of people who have learned much from popular culture. Even though most people are not intensely involved in politics, both their occasional participation in and imagination of politics is affected by their popular experience. People do not categorically separate politics from the rest of their experience, so popular culture becomes for them an important source of imaginative and participatory conceptions. Politics is inseparable from the conduct of popular discourse, in that aspects of culture are interwoven into the fabric of people's ongoing experience, contribution to the continual weaving of the social tapestry.

In this way, people's experience with political culture is aesthetic. Political culture is imagined in terms of myths, symbols, and values, and participated in terms of one's conception of what politics is like and what one's obligations and efficacy might be. We like to see politics as a drama, and evaluate what happens there as dramatic critics using aesthetic criteria. Political actors are judged by the quality of their performances, events and projects by their dramatic satisfaction, and contests by dramatic choice. As popular culture becomes more pervasive and powerful, we are more attentive to the conventions of a *popular aesthetic*, the ways in which we evaluate our immediate experience, and relate it to other realms, such as politics. Politics is a dramatic realm for most of us, an insubstantial pageant of heroes, villains, and fools, an arena of action beyond our mundane lives. But it is not beyond our evaluation, which tends to be aesthetic since our comprehension of politics is by necessity vicarious. Popular culture helps us to "know" politics through our imaginative powers.

Let us return again to the objects of play in childhood. We noted that play with dolls is a culturally-related experience, one that teaches attitudes that might become part of a maturing adult's expectations about the world. Suppose that in childhood a child spends a great deal of playtime with war toys and games. From a very early age, little boys and girls in the United States play with G.I. Joe and allies in mock combat against identifiable foes (terrorists, drug dealers), Rambo dolls, He-man and Masters of the Universe, Captain Power and Soldiers of the Future, and so on. War toy lines include a great deal of futuristic "high-tech" military hardware—airplanes, missiles, tanks, ships, and space attack vehicles. Many television cartoon shows aimed at children are based upon lines of war toys. Too, kids can play war games at the mall arcade or on their TV. Now there are interactive games with computerized capabilities so that when a kid makes a "kill" on the TV screen it activates toys in the living room which are also "destroyed" (ejecting enemy soldiers from a tank and the like). A walk through a contemporary large toy store reveals an arsenal of toy weapons (assault rifles, for instance). A glance into children's rooms and you will notice that war imagery is not confined just to toys, but is apparent on pajamas, sheets, posters, lunchboxes, T-shirts, you name it. War toys are pervasive in our children's popular culture. Every day millions of children engage in play-violence and pay-killing.[5]

For a long time, there has been a debate as to whether playing war teaches children to be more aggressive and violence-prone. War toys, critics charge, make war seem attractive, heroic, and decisive; war games make killing seem painless, combat fun, and war altogether not really dangerous. Others think war play just a healthy outlet for energy, or defend war toys as a market choice (by one figure, over $1.1 billion spent on them in 1986 alone). From the point of view developed here, however, children might get multiple meanings out of play with war toys, or perhaps even no lasting meaning at all; a toy can just be a toy. Nor does it have to be the case that someone intends to make kids more warlike; toymakers may not have a hidden agenda in league with the war industry to produce a new generation of willing young warriors ready to fight. It also may be impossible to conclusively demonstrate that war play in early childhood makes young adults into good soldiers and affects their willingness to kill on a battlefield, since there are so many other intervening factors and such a time gap between play and reality.

But we can say that popular play with war toys is an aesthetic experience that includes the potential for politically-relevant learning. When kids play war, they are dramatizing in their imagination the use of force in order to achieve individual and group purposes. The play-world they imagine is metaphorical, in that they are understanding something from the world beyond their normal purview by vicarious experience in play. They are thus understanding something from political culture in terms of a "substitutionary" activity, play with popular culture. If the life lesson learned in that activity is that war is fun, victorious, and worthwhile, then political learning has taken place, so affecting subsequent attitudes and action. War has been accorded symbolic legitimation in the minds of children who will grow up to be citizens and soldiers. There will be in their lives many other supportive and conflicting messages about war, but we cannot discount as unimportant widespread play with the war-objects of popular culture.

The sources of continuity and change in political culture, then, must include political learning from popular culture. Popular culture is play with ways of seeing the world, and thus can eventually influence how we act toward the world. Further, as we live as adults in the dynamic world of politics, popular culture can continue to serve us as a source of knowledge and action. Popular culture relates to politics as it unfolds, by aesthetic reactions to political tides and trends, moods and rhythms. The creators of popular culture can even at times anticipate political developments. The marketing of toys, for example, may be a decision undertaken with a future "political climate" in mind. But in any case the "immediate experience" of popular culture helps us to orient ourselves towards the temper of the times. This can range from popular novels to television evangelists to theme parks, but in all instances popular experience has the potential to aid us in understanding political time. The political story of a time (the "New Deal," the "Eisenhower normalcy," the "Reagan Era") is eventually interwoven into the cultural tapestry through popular interpretation of how "our time" relates to the whole story, the *mythos* of the political culture as it persists through time.

The American Myth

The political culture of the United States is rooted in a fundamental and persistent myth, a cultural folktale often called "The American Dream." It is a quest myth, a story of a "new world" that holds out the promise of human perfection as the "last, best hope" of humankind. America came to be seen as the "virgin land" wherein nature and civilization would meet together in a union of barbaric energy and democratic society, creating a "new sacred order." The mythos of the Dream supported stories of individual achievement in a culture of equality and opportunity, wherein the "simple genuine self" of the American Adam, girded with a "wiser innocence," can then actively build the promised land. The definition of what that land would look like has made the Dream a pluralistic myth, and for some the Dream has turned into a nightmare. But the Dream persists, given ever new retelling.[6]

The interplay of popular and political culture occurs in the dynamic context of the myth of cultural quest. We do not merely quest as individuals, we quest as a nation. America has a destiny that impels us towards its completion, the myth says, sustaining our national will to believe over time. The national adventure of the United States is an odyssey with a mission, a passage across frontiers towards a state of perfection. Even though national values were "given" at the outset in our mythic acts of foundation, we are still hindered by lapses and obstacles in the present that obstruct our passage into destined perfection. These exigencies are the dragons to be slain on the hero's quest, the evils that threaten to thwart the manifestation of our destiny, the flaws in ourselves that make us doubt whether the quest will end in triumph. But in both political and popular imagery, we have recurrently foreseen a future in which the promise of American life has been fulfilled. The American Dream may remain a shimmering mirage on the horizon of our collective life, but its promise gives renewed vigor to valuing and pursuing the quest, producing cultural heroes who exemplify and lead us, we hope, toward realization of our mythic aspiration.

In both political and popular culture, the American quest to establish the Dream is rooted in and transmitted across generations by the stories we tell about seeking and finding our promised destiny. The American myth is variously told, but we contend that in the ongoing tradition of our national imagination political and popular imagery resonates around the vision of three related communities. These mythic communities have taken many imaginary forms, but they add up to a resemblance of what the American Dream would look like if it were to be realized. These are a moral community, which is the realm of our cultural ideals expressed in institutions such as family, church, and school; a material community, the realm of economic ideals based on the value of work and the goal of the creation of deserved individual wealth and worthwhile social wealth in the legitimate activities of a commercial civilization; and a political community, the realm of political ideals of democratic self-government and sturdy republican institutions exemplified not only in the monumental landmarks of the nation's capital but also in our imagination of the perfection of community. These three mythical communities can be conceived separately, and on a macrocosmic or microcosmic scale, but in functional combination they add up to the American myth of the sought and destined community of our national imagination.[7]

The image of these three mythic communities are all of political relevance. If at a particular time we are telling ourselves stories about lapses or barriers in the quest for community, this involves a cultural and temporal perception that we are lacking in some way as to our resolve or ability to achieve the promised Dream. Stories might then revolve around the tension between moral poverty and moral prosperity, material poverty and material prosperity, or political poverty and political prosperity, and of course combinations among these. For instance, if we look at the movies of the early 1930's, a common theme is the existence of material poverty among the many, but moral poverty among the rich few; the spunky many (journalists, showgirls, domestic servants, and so on) possess the moral prosperity of democratic folk wisdom, though none of the wealth of the morally bankrupt rich, who are sometimes silly and out of touch and in other instances venal and narrow-minded. When the political community is depicted, it is shown as in a state of political poverty—corrupt big city machines, cigar-chomping courthouse gangs, hostile and violent cops and railroad goons, heartless judges, and brutal prisons and reform schools. However, with the advent of the New Deal, the political community is accorded a new status, with G-men as heroes, reformers running prisons and rehabilitating prisoners, kids given hope of a normal life beyond slums and reform school, judges becoming benevolent, and Okies given hope by the Farm Security Administration. By the late Thirties, there is an identifiable perception of renewed political prosperity, and the re-emergence of hopes of the spread of moral and material prosperity sponsored by a benevolent government that has recovered its political legitimacy. The interplay of movie representations of these aspects of the American myth occurred in the urgent context of the Depression and New Deal, offering us popular evidence of the salience of, and lapses in, our quest for completion of the Dream.

This book is about the confluence of American popular and political life, understood largely through those popular expressions which offer evidence of the cultural relationship. American politics occurs in the interwoven fabric of popular life, and cannot be fully understood without reference to its popular context. The popular as well as the political expressions of American myth, as manifest in stories that emerge in a given historical time, can be usefully interpreted to enhance our understanding of the dynamics of American politics. Our mythic quest here is to increase the amount of political understanding in the world.

To that end, the book will be divided into two parts. The first part will deal with American popular dramas as they become manifest in popular activity that "bubbles up" in play. This includes popular folklore transmitted in interpersonal communication, but which also become the fare of popular media. Too, we will consider the persistence of popular legends, focusing on the Western myth and its political meaning. Thirdly, we will deal with popular sports as a form of folk drama, including what cultural meaning still inheres in sports even today. Finally, we will treat popular religion as a form of popular activity that has become a potent cultural and political force. The second part of the book will examine popular media and the "media culture," pointing to how the media participate in popular politics through the ideas and images they communicate to mass audiences. Media messages "trickle down" to us, shaping our political imagination through their dramatic representations. So here we will examine in turn, first, the depiction and reporting of politics by the popular media. Secondly, we will look at the popular art of American political propaganda. Then we will discuss the relationship between show business and politics, especially the phenomenon of celebrity. Finally, we will look at the spread of popular culture around the world and the political impact it is having. By the end of this quest, the reader hopefully will see the dimensions of the relationship between popular culture and politics, and leave the book better able to understand both the popular and political world in which she or he lives.

Part I
American Popular Dramas and Politics

An Introductory Note

It has become a common, and powerful, argument in recent years that popular culture is produced. The "production of culture" school maintains, following the Frankfurt School, that the "culture industry" is the source and arbiter of popular culture, controlling the means of cultural production and communication, and therefore exercising "hegemony" over the cultural experience of the masses. In many ways, this critical position is quite correct, and in the second half of the book we will return to it for its explanatory power. But it should be counterbalanced with the view that popular culture is ultimately the culture of the populace, and that the populace plays an active role in selecting and using culture for its own purposes. It is true that those elites that control the production of culture exercise great and perhaps often preponderant influence over cultural selection and utilization, delimiting popular choice to those cultural objects and activities that are available. But here as in political and economic relations, the interplay between elite and mass is transactional, complex, and changing. The advent of cable television expanded both elite control and mass choice over what to watch on television, and made for seredipitious innovations such as the rise of televangelism and independent programming. We might call cultural relations in relatively free societies one of popular negotiation, with both elite producers and mass consumers seeking what the former hopes and the latter actually finds desirable.

So in the first part of this book, we will look at forms of popular thought and action with clear popular origins, on the theory that such clusters of popular thinking and acting have widespread democratic roots and then "bubble up" into elite sponsorship. Even though popular folklore, popular folktales such as the Western, popular sports, and popular religion eventually become the

18

institutional province of elite powers. But even then, they endure because of their popular appeal, evidenced by widespread popular interest about, and participation in, what had begun as a folk belief or activity. Baseball began in cow pastures and sandlots, and developed into a lucrative institutionalized professional sport; but it survives because of its popular power at both local and professional levels, from Little League to Major League. Such persistent cultural activities, at both mass and elite levels, retain and perpetuate politically significant meanings in the form of popular dramas. Central to the logic of a popular order is the habit of people participating in, either in actual or vicarious involvement, dramas which celebrate popular myths. Myths are the first-order beliefs of a political culture in story form, and popular myths are the democratic, or folkish, version of cultural mythology. Popular forms such as sports and westerns fulfill a need for the dramatic celebration of myths in the ritualized, or formulaic, settings of recognizable plays. It is our contention here that these popular expressions are evidence of widespread attitudes and expectations that are relevant to the conduct of politics, since they indicate the mythic and dramatistic basis of political culture. At this level, it is the people who are producing culture.

In a purely folk culture, the people would have to depend upon traditional media of popular communications—storytellers, troubadors and bards, griots and shaman, and so on. But in a "media culture," we have pervasive and sophisticated modern means of popular communication. What we are interested in there by shifting focus to elite organizations that produce culture is the extent to which that popular mythology, as depicted in mass mediated dramas, creates and transforms popular culture, and by extension, helps to shape attitudes and expectations about politics. So in the second part of the book, we will examine the media culture as a vehicle of popular messages with political relevance. In the first part of the book, then, we will attribute power to the people as the arbiters of popular expression and its political consequences; in the second half, we will attribute power to the media as the purveyors of expressions that have both popular and political consequences. The distinction is not arbitrary, allowing us to examine the sources and uses to which popular culture is put by both elites and masses. It helps us to remember that popular culture is continually recreated and changed in the interplay of those who produce culture among both cultural elites who dominate institutions and cultural masses who dominate opinion. In the final analysis, both need each other, and the cultural transaction is ongoing and constantly renegotiated. And this process of negotiation occurs in the dynamic context of politics, the interplay of which is our subject here.

Chapter Two
Popular Folk Heritage and American Politics

The Flow of Popular Discourse

Students of public opinion have long recognized that there are aspects of popular knowledge—the feelings, thoughts, and attitudes of the many—that are difficult to understand or measure. Public opinion polls offer only superficial insight into the depths of popular knowledge, and indeed are only a momentary reflection of what is an ongoing process. For the discourse of the populace, especially in a political culture wherein people feel relatively free to think or talk as they wish, is a dynamic form of knowing that helps to shape how people react to politics and politicians. Popular knowing is often quite different, and more colorful and unpredictable, than elite knowledge of political and social affairs. The "popular mind," to use the metaphor of the subjective experience of many millions of people, is oftentimes uninformed by elite standards. But in a democratic society where everyone's vote counts one, and the power of public opinion is great, politicians seeking electoral and popular support in office find the popular mind a necessary object of study. When the fictional politician Willie Stark (based on Huey Long) of Robert Penn Warren's novel *All the King's Men* had as his slogan, "My study is the heart of the people," he understood that the popular mind is at the base of democratic politics.

The popular mind has some knowledge of the past, immediate experiences in the present, and an image of the future. This knowledge is culled and interpreted as a "strategy for living," providing people with ideas and images of pragmatic use in everyday life and in evaluating more remote and puzzling processes such as politics. Such knowledge may be a traditional source learned early in life, such as patriotic catechism that teaches national values and reverence for symbols (the flag) and icons (George Washington). Another great American source is the Bible, from which people

21

have drawn values, stories, and aphorisms applicable to explaining contemporary problems, including political ones. Such sources of popular knowledge may have official sanction, but they may be used by the populace in very unofficial ways. The Bible, for instance, has been pointed to as authoritative justification for racial segregation, the subordination of women, corporal punishment of children, and violent revenge against our enemies, stigmatized as agents of Satan. Elites may point to the Bible, or other traditional sources of popular knowledge, for rhetorical purposes, but segments of the mass may find the same sources justification for a political agenda or choices.

The same may be said for national history. Historians and journalists, armed with their critical methods and debunking facts, may portray an American history that bears the realistic whips and scorns of open-eyed inquiry. But many people wish to see their nation's history in more romantic terms, as a grand and progressive drama towards some historical destiny. Critical history comes to be seen (by, for instance, local folks who concern themselves with the thrust of high school history books) as not history the way it should be, a folktale that validates the commonplace desire to believe in the historical romance of one's own country. Tales of massacres by the good guys (from Wounded Knee to My Lai), slavery and prejudice, exploitation and greed all are brutal facts that invalidate the beautiful theory of national rectitude. Children are not learning popular history, on which it is thought there should be consensus as to the norm of ethnocentric self-congratulation. With the conflict of norms, history texts for public schools become a battleground over tone and content, and often end up being a puerile mishmash of no interest to students.

Further, our conceptions of history are complemented, or even wholly derived, from our popular experience with mass-mediated representations. For decades, Hollywood has long produced historical dramas, in a wide variety of exotic settings. But in most cases, the past is dramatized in a way palatable for popular audiences at a particular time and taste culture. So, for instance, generations grew up imagining Biblical stories as Hollywood portrayed them, although those portrayals were favorably received because they gave popular life (including sex, violence, and spectacle) to favorite Biblical stories. Like popular tales about American history, people enjoyed fictional additions to the Bible, as with eternally popular fictive tales such as *Ben-hur* and *The Robe*. Stories from traditional sources persist as part of the popular fund of discourse, reappearing in every generation in new form, adapting such folktales for new exigencies as they appear. Figures such as Jesus or Washington will acquire new popular meaning in different political eras: in the 1980s, Jesus re-emerged as a stern conservative with a punitive social agenda, and Washington was refurbished as a model of rectitude and piety.

At the base of democratic politics and social life, then, is the *flow of popular discourse*. When we say that this discourse is the province of "the folk," we mean this in terms of the modern anthropology of experience, whereby ordinary people become the mediators of much of what we take to be reality. The imaginative life of masses of people is communicated over time, perpetuating and changing widespread ideas and images of the world. So when we speak of folklore, we have in mind not archaic tales that were told in a premodern world and are now of only antiquarian interest. Rather we are concerned with the living talk and storytelling of people as they cope with the burdens and puzzles of contemporary life in all its organizational and technological complexity. Modern folk are no less "folkish" in their playful interest in and use of popular discourse, that like all folklore, helps them understand and adapt to the world in which they live. Too, the lore of the folk also is instrumental in the formation of folkways, those habits of mind and action that help people orient themselves towards the world.

One of the most universal and astonishing of modern folklore widely distributed among the mass population are "urban legends." These are stories, many of which persist over long periods of time in various forms, that are believed to be recent, but which belie some widespread anxiety about the contemporary world. They are "true" in the apocryphal sense, in that they illustrate something important about the dangers and opportunities of modern life. There may be alligators in the sewers; poisonous snakes lurking in the imported carpets at K-Mart; worm meat in the hamburgers at McDonalds; and drugged babysitters who microwave and eat your child while you are at a party. But, according to similar legends, you may also fall into a golden opportunity such as the fellow who bought a new Porsche for $50, sold by a revengeful wife whose husband ran off with his secretary and told her to sell the car and send him the money; or take a class from the lecherous and beautiful female professor who selected one male student per class for extracurricular sexual instruction, grading him on an average of his classroom and bedroom performances. Such folktales never happened to anyone, but they do speak to mass fantasies about what could happen, specifically in the current world.[1]

Another category closely related to urban legends are the larger and older tales that seem to enjoy popular salience, stories of unsolved mysteries and forces in the world that may affect us. The folktale of "The Vanishing Hitchhiker," for instance, goes back well into the nineteenth century, and has been told in many countries and continents. The story of the homicidal maniac "Hook" and "The Dead Boyfriend" are also ancient and ubiquitous. Such old tales are often told in new form, as with the stories about "new age" religious cults alleged to engage in satanic practices such as baby sacrifice. If something virtually unprecedented appears, such as the AIDS epidemic, old stories about fatal and highly communicable diseases are revived, not to mention anti-gay jokes that suggest they might deserve their fate. Legends develop again as to the various bizarre ways one can contract AIDS, and the unorthodox and threatening activities of religious groups deemed "cults." Lore persists in both talk and tabloid about the Bermuda triangle, the Abominable Snowman and Bigfoot, the power of the Great Pyramid, and flying saucers.[2]

Folklore persists about the recurrent appearance of and communication with extra-terrestials, whose purposes have ranged from the extremes of malevolence and benevolence. In the latter case, science-fictionists have catered to the mass fantasy that god-like beings (updating our belief in angels or other benevolent powers from beyond Earth) have arrived to bring us good tidings and superior wisdom, suggesting a latent mass feeling that perhaps we cannot cope on our own without the help of scientific alien gods. In the former instance, the alien fantasy "displaces" fears about malevolent superior beings taking us over or destroying us. After a century of popular thought, translated into science-fiction expressions, belief in extra-terrestials has become an integral part of our popular folklore. In moments of stress among those who are impressionable and panicky, such a belief can manifest itself in reaction. On Halloween eve, 1938, Orson Welles broadcast over the radio a recreation of H.G. Wells' *The War of the Worlds* in the format of an urgent news broadcast that had interrupted normal programming. Although most listeners recognized the program as fictional, there were some people who believed it to be an account of a real invasion from Mars and acted upon it, fleeing, crying, praying, arming themselves, and so on. These scared folks were the victims of their own imaginations, activated by the theme in popular thought that envisioned menacing bogeymen from outer space, and made salient by the anxieties of the historical moment, with very real bogeymen—the Nazis—threatening invasion from the Mars of Germany.[3]

Popular thought may acquire political relevance in a wide variety of more subtle and implicit ways. If "tabloid talk" convinces us that the world is a corrupt and exploitative place, then this will give credence to an attitude that politics is part of that world, and thus should be viewed with suspicion and contempt. On the other hand, if we are heir to a legacy of stories to which we attribute cultural significance, we may develop expectations that political figures should possess certain qualities, and that political situations should have certain outcomes. Let us look at two profoundly American popular themes: the expected life-cycle of heroes, and the captivity narrative.

The Myth of the Hero

Popular discourse and knowledge may be immediate in its interest, but in any ongoing culture, it has mythic roots. By myth we mean not a "false belief" but rather a long-lasting and deeply ingrained folktale or representation that dramatizes important themes in our political culture, and possesses not literal but rather apocryphal truth. We may hypothesize that for large populations myth is a "deep structure" of more significance than "ideology," if we mean by that term the logic of ideas. It may be the case that the American populace does not have an articulate and "forensic" ideology in the sense of a coherent intellectual position on government and politics. But people do respond to stories which activate patriotic or "common sense" notions, combining idea with image in narrative form, an imaginative popular form that has been called "ideographs." An ideograph, in that sense, is not devoid of culturally derived and politically important ideas, only that it becomes manifest in popularly acceptable motifs. The ideological position concerning the proper relationship between effort and reward so dominant in American political culture is rarely discussed in popular circles in abstract terms. But in the past it was given popular formulation in the Horatio Alger books, the long tradition of self-help literature that caters to fantasies of monetary or psychic riches, children's stories (such as "The Little Engine That Could"), and in the group dynamics of popular talk (tales of welfare cheaters driving Cadillacs). At an ideological level, the defense of wealth through individual achievement and the attack on the unsuccessful as unworthy is a tenet of conservative thought. But at the level of popular narrative, we are witnessing the imagination of what we should believe and how we should live. As an ideograph, we are in the realm of "the folklore of capitalism" as it is mediated through popular communication, with potentially powerful political consequences in terms of the influence of public opinion on policy and the appeals made by voting choices.[4]

Popularly-derived conceptions of the world includes what constitutes cultural heroism. A popular hero has characteristics and career that conform with the logic of a popular society, as told in the mythology of heroism. It is usual for heroes to be so because they have a popular following, becoming for those followers a personage who represents something of symbolic importance to the culture at a given time. For example, John William Ward's studies of Andrew Jackson and Charles Lindbergh pointed out that such figures became "symbolic leaders" for their followers because they represented certain values at the right moment. Jackson emerged as the heroic representation of the achievements and aspirations of the fledgling country in its dynamic moment of proud nationalism and optimistic expansion. Lindbergh became an heroic sensation through his flight of the Atlantic, dramatizing the possibility of individual heroic action (he flew alone) in a new technological age that threatened to become patently unheroic through the pervasion of organizational conformity. He became a folk hero of the industrial age, as someone who displayed the adventurous spirit characteristic of premodern figures striding into an unknown like Daniel Boone, but who also mastered the mystery of a new technology that will loft us into the future. In that sense, popular heroes combine aspects of both past and future, giving their admirers hope that the heroic qualities inherited from the past will not be lost, and that those qualities will be adequate to face and conquer the brave new world of the future.[5]

When one comes to political heroism, however, there are some special problems and opportunities. Political heroes are often derivative: their heroism was shaped in some other field of endeavor—business, farming, law, war, education, or popular entertainment, including astronauts, popular heroes clearly in the Lindbergh tradition. The extent to which political candidates— such as George Bush and Robert Dole—played up their war records (and in Dole's case, wound) suggests the continued salience of the aspiring political hero's participation in a mythic time. The American Presidency from Eisenhower to Bush was still deeply wedded to the heroic folklore of World War II, suggesting the extent to which we were still committed as a nation to the feat of winning the war (and clinging to the myth that we alone won it). The ironic turn in world history in the 1990s that seemed to make the United States and the Soviet Union the eventual losers and Japan and Germany the eventual winners of World War II likely made us cling to that mythic time all the more ardently. Although others (Lyndon Johnson, for example) represented themselves as a folk hero because they were close to the soil, as agrarian culture receded from national memory the traditional appeal to rustic heroism (that one is "a simple old country boy") one saw last in figures such as Sam Ervin began to fade. Business heroics still had its lure in some quarters, but if business continues to acquire a bad reputation after so much scandal, it might become as suspect as a source of political heroics as law and medicine.

It was the field of popular entertainment as an area of achievement that was most intriguing, especially after the political success of Ronald Reagan. Reagan's first career as a movie actor had established his celebrity, if not his outstanding acting talent; but his second career, as Governor of California and then President, was notable for his ability to place himself as someone of virtually mythic origins and experience, conversant with primal truths and folkish beliefs which he carried and expressed to a new age. He represented himself as a figure from some prelapsarian age who would bring the canons of popular knowledge to a fallen world. His mastery of folklore included the famous apocryphal tales that weren't literally true but illustrated some political moral for our time. He conjured up sports tales, stories of village kindness, barnraisings, Huck Fynn idylls, Air Force flyers going down in flames with their wounded buddy (how Reagan knew is unclear), the wisdom of businessmen and the idiocy of government, welfare queens buying vodka with food stamps, Indians getting rich on reservation oil, and so on endlessly. Reagan was virtually a walking encyclopedia of popular folklore, made politically potent by its application to the conduct of government. Reagan expanded the role of the Presidency to include chief folklorist, opening a whole new ethnographic field of inquiry. But more importantly, he demonstrated through the "acceptance" of these apocryphal tales by audiences of various composition a widespread mass yearning for mythic reaffirmation. Those moved by Reagan's folktales of American heroic rectitude and daring had every reason to know that they weren't true in any literal sense. But in the wake of historical disillusionment during the late twentieth century, the rhetorical celebration of America as a once and future power of noble intent and heroic destiny was a temptation Americans could not resist. Bush also made much of this deep popular desire for national justification by faith, but how long belief could be sustained in the rapid flow of political change was impossible to tell.[6]

Indeed, as America drifts into the "post-modern" world, the media culture has become so pervasive that folk heroism, although originating in folkish traditions, can quickly be captured and transformed by popular attention that attracts the mass media. Further, for several decades now the origins and nature of folk heroism has become blurred by its immediate encapsulation by the media. The eminent folklorist Richard Dorson made the distinction between "folklore" and "fakelore," the former being an authentic popular expression and the latter being "the voice not of the folk but of the mass culture." In politics, the folk and the fake have been mixed up for a very long time, since folk beliefs, emotions, and stories have been exploited by politicians wishing to appeal to them. Democratic flattery is one of the oldest campaign ploys. The "log cabin" myth, for instance, is at least as old as Andrew Jackson and about as new as Jesse Jackson. Studies of official campaign biographies have demonstrated the continued featuring of the democratic myth of humble origins from which the candidate rises through heroic achievement to well-deserved recognition and approval. Jimmy Carter's *Why Not the Best* and Reagan's *Where's the Rest of Me?* play upon this resilient myth, translated into campaign propaganda to assure voters of the candidate's native origins and therefore wisdom (candidates who were born rich, such as George Bush and John F. Kennedy, had to stress other things). However, now we may wonder under what circumstances the log cabin myth might survive, or whether it is now becoming almost wholly a creature of political fabrication. If it does survive, it will be with candidates such as Jesse Jackson, who will appeal to their origins not only in poverty but in discrimination; but what will candidates do who were born in modal circumstances of the affluent suburb?

Even though the folkish belief in the necessity and characteristics of heroes may change (to include, for example, women and blacks), we may wonder if heroism is being more fundamentally transformed by mass experience with play. Historians have gained evidence about the transformation of the hero into a celebrity, and how that focus on "idols of production" (businessmen, lawyers, bankers) was superseded by "idols of consumption" (athletes, movie stars, cafe society). But in the late twentieth century, these category shifts have become blurred—heroism and celebrity go hand in hand with a figure like Reagan, and Donald Trump may be for his admirers a hero of production and a celebrity of consumption. But in this changed social climate, the power of such figures stems from their ability to command popular attention, be it admiration or disdain. Reagan exercised leadership both in his sponsorship of business values through policy and rhetoric, and his personal representation of the benefits of such advocacy in an opulent and expensive lifestyle (much of which was paid for by the taxpayers). Trump was both celebrated and condemned for his corporate buccaneering and public display of his self-important attitude and the gilded cages in which he lived. In these and many other instances the power of public figures stemmed from their popularity, whether it was positive notability or negative notoriety. The logic of a popular society gives impetus to an array of popular heroes, villains, and fools, all of whom are so regarded because of their *status as figures of popular play.*

Heroes were once characterized by their great deeds, and the reputation for heroic qualities that flowed from real accomplishment. Such a figure was an "event-making" personage whose life and example made a discernable difference in history, and evoked popular reactions because of his or her heroic actions. But now heroes are "eventful," figures whose heroic being is more of a result of popular play than by anything they may have done. To be sure, the relationship is transactional, with both hero and followers needing and creating each other. But whereas before a hero committed deeds and then became an object of folklore, now a hero creates his or her own folklore and then becomes heroic (or villainous or foolish). We may illustrate this by comparing George Washington and Ronald Reagan. Washington was a leader in the tradition of Cincinnatus, reluctant but stalwart, the "indispensable man" who represented in act and bearing the ideals of the revolution and the new republic. He thereby became a genuine object of admiration, and the subject of considerable popular folklore, including Parson Weems' infamous cherry tree treatment. Reagan was more in the tradition of Hollywood, which called for stars to be cultural and now political leaders, as actors who communicate public espousal of national values rather than as people of action who defend and further them in war and peace. Like other political celebrities, Reagan was complicit in creating his own heroic myth, which was more of a product of adroit self-promotion and image management than prior heroic accomplishment. He was a latter-day media figure who was a celebrity before he became a self-made hero, creating his own folklore through propaganda. Washington was a Whig hero who exemplified the principles of conservative republicanism; Reagan was a ludenic hero who exemplified the principles of popular celebrity enacting a heroic role on a public stage. In Washington's case, popular folklore about his followed the trail of his public career and persisted in national memory after his death, elevating him to heroic apotheosis; in Reagan's case, folklore was used by him and created about him to further his public career, but likely to be as ephemeral as his heroism.[8]

We may well live, then, in the age of the *ludenic hero*, figures who acquire public status rather than achieve public deeds. They are figures of popular play rather than the creations of heroic work. They may well achieve things in business, sports, entertainment, or whatever; but their status in well-knownness is an acquisition they seek through the manipulation of popular knowledge, creating a folklore about them. Washington achieved national fame through deeds that made him "first in the hearts of his countrymen," a figure central to our political heritage. Popular figures of the ludenic age are by contrast heroes for the moment, since their fame (or infamy) is rooted in nothing more than celebrity, and thus their place in history as achiever and exemplar is more ephemeral. Figures of play, however powerful in their moment, are subject to the whims of popular attention, fading from social memory quickly. The story of someone like Washington endures in folk memory through the didactic retelling of his story; the story of someone like Reagan evaporates from folk memory because it is a tale without folk roots or memorable lesson. The traditional hero was largely a creature of the real events that he or she mastered, becoming the stuff of legend; the ludenic hero is largely a self-creation of the media events through which they commanded momentary attention. Both are figures of the popular imagination, but the former endures through their substantial presence in national memory, while the latter fades through inanition, lacking a quality of substance.

In a ludenic age, political heroes, villains, and folks come and go quickly, since popular attention span is short and fickle. Since such figures create their own folklore, or use their own public story to spread their fame, the mass public consumes it with the same attitude it takes toward other media figures, being amused by the apparition momentarily holding their attention and then discarding it for other shapes that supersede it. Reagan's appeal to a wide variety of folkish themes and stories made his tenure as a ludenic hero longer than most, but even in his case, interest began to fade after the Iran-contra affair, and after he left office seemed to have left no enduring impression as public attention shifted elsewhere. A creature of media play must accept the consequences of being the object of "instant folklore" and the mutual exploitation of actor and audience under way: the actor exploits folkish themes from the common culture in order to give credence and legitimacy to his or her act, and the audience exploits the actor by enjoying the mediated use of folklore in the conduct of the act. Reagan's self-identification with insular (the heartland "childhood home" in Dixon, Illinois), militaristic ("Semper Fi"), and other symbols of the popular civil religion brought immediate political benefit, but carved no lasting political monument.

Ludenic heroism, then, has severe limits as a political strategy. By tending to turn folklore into fakelore, it makes the common political heritage of lore and legend into just another consumable, as immediate and disposable as any other bought object of amusement or pleasure. Folklore comes to be seen as both rootless and exploitable, as something that offers us no link to the past, but is used to stir vague memories of emotionally-charged symbols of national culture for immediate political purposes. Perhaps the most fundamental aspect of the heroic tradition in the United States is *the hero's quest*. Indeed, the story of the heroic adventure of a cultural representative carrying out a redemptive task for the community may be one of the most universal and persistent of all mythemes. In its American version, it has tended to be a folktale featuring an indigenous hero whose rise to power and mighty acts are selflessly done for the community from which he (and sometimes she) springs and acts on behalf of the many who are themselves helpless. Like all heroism, there is something patently undemocratic about such popular legends, but nevertheless we are recurrently drawn to the renewed story of someone with superior powers who will save us. This tale has been aptly termed "the American monomyth," and its political relevance is also revived from time to time.[9]

In politics, the hero's quest will often appear as the basic mytheme in a candidate for high office's public life story. In official campaign biographies, convention films, and the candidate's acceptance speech, the candidate for President or whatever is self-portrayed as a person of the people, someone who either through humble origins or notable achievement (including a war record, business success, feats in public service) acquires the heroic abilities that qualifies him or her as a personage of destiny. Andrew Jackson was the first Presidential contender for whom this popular legend was widely ballyhooed; but it has become a staple of campaign propaganda ever since. Nor is it confined just to campaigning, self-casting the candidate as fitting the heroic mold, and living out the hero's quest. Since popular heroes are "symbolic leaders," in a ludenic age they can emerge and disappear quickly, but in the meantime acquire a reputation and a following. Lindbergh again was a pioneer of ludenic heroism at the beginning of the proliferation of mass media: immediately after the fact, he was acclaimed a hero who had completed his quest, and now had to be accorded the acclaim and deference we should all demonstrate. His flight of the Atlantic became an instant legend through mass communication, and his heroism was defined as the feature of the story that made for the completion of the quest. Since Lindbergh, other figures have become immediate popular heroes, and some have been much more astute users of the mass media in such self-definition.[10]

Such was the case with the short but meteoric ludenic career of Oliver North. The Iran-contra scandal was a complex and puzzling affair, with the national security elite scrambling to survive damaging revelations about covert operations that were illegal at best and stupid at worst. However, unlike Watergate, the major elite figures in the affair—the President and the national security functionaries involved—did manage to finesse the investigation through adroit management, aided by the emergence of a media figure who focused and diverted attention on himself as a hero wronged. Oliver North became an instant hero through dramatic self-presentation, casting himself as a hero on a quest thwarted by small-minded and niggardly little men in the Presidential bureaucracy and the Congress. The quest was vague but proclaimed (in North's testimony before Congress) as patriotic and selfless, a risky and daring adventure that would kill two terrors with one stone, Iranian-backed hostage-takers and the Nicaraguan Sandanistas. North appealed to our desire for individual heroism in a world full of threatening and untouchable villains abroad, and the frustrations of legal and bureaucratic constraints at home. In his testimony and speeches, he seemed able to have it both ways, claiming he was "only following orders" of now cowardly institutional leaders (including President Reagan), but in the truly decisive way of the independent hero, also able to defy normal constraints and act on his own. He self-cast himself as the betrayed loyal servant now set up to be the fall guy, and like the sheriff abandoned by the town in *High Noon*, the only one left out there in the cold fighting against the forces of evil. And like Mr. Smith going to Washington, he now was the only one with the heroic guts to tell the story of his heroism and its betrayal. North appealed to the tradition of heroic single combat, of the hero alone against all odds and all cowardice, willing to go "one on one" against an infamous Arab terrorist and able to see the Big Picture clearly, an ability lost on official Washington. At that moment, North had the same appeal as the fictional Rambo, fighting against enemies both foreign and domestic, the villains abroad who he stood against like Horatio at the bridge, and the fools in the Establishment who would not act against a clear and present danger.

Although North proved to be a passing public fancy, he captured the moment by becoming a mass-mediated ludenic hero with whom large audiences could play without responsibility or consequences. A ludenic hero exists as a creature of amusement, although like North, he or she may appeal to long-extant and widely held national folklore. But in a complicated and patently unheroic present, it becomes playfully easy for mass audiences to focus on a lone figure like North, representing what should be done now in accordance with the logic of single heroism, but without any widespread expectation that North, or anyone else, will be able in fact to do what the hero said needed to be done. But mass media audiences are fickle and impatient, and after enjoying Ollie's telegenic performance, both interest in him and approval of him began to wane. (His approval ratings in public opinion polls dropped from 53% in 1987 to 39% in 1988, and the television docudrama on him, "Guts and Glory," was clobbered in the ratings.) Such is the fate of ludenic heroes: both Reagan and North quickly became ephemeral after they were out of sight, since their power was limited to their ability to command attention, rather than direct policies or armies. North, like Reagan, came into purview by arousing memories of our folk heroic legacy, now delimited to being a part of our media experience. This is not to say that ludenic heroes are fakelore, only that they are heroes of play for audiences used to observing media heroism and responding to play-heroism. Ludenic heroes are complemented by ludenic villains and fools who may be equally "real-life" characters (e.g., Khaddafi, Noriega) but who are altercasted as such through the logic of popular mediation, becoming "villainous" only through successful characterization as worthy foils for the hero. Khaddafi and Noriega are "barbarian" characters familiar in our national folklore as dark threats to the peaceable community, and who must be thwarted by the hero. But they are no less objects of play, fitting the folkish mold as adequate villains, and getting their just deserts in military raids that display heroic resolve for media audiences. All ludenic figures are subject to the canons and habits of the media world that communicates, and constrains, their heroism, drawing from folklore but making them part of a more insubstantial world.[11]

Long ago philosopher David Hume noted that the true source of power was in the will of those who supported the one who exercised power. Opinion, then, is the base of power, but opinion can take different forms. Hume distinguished between the opinion of right (I consent to power because whomever exercises it is legitimate) and opinion of interest (I consent to power because it will pay me to). In the media age, we add the importance of the *opinion of amusement*. Now people are drawn to consent to power because whomever exercises it is amusing, playful, and attractive, able to sway us into being an attentive audience who are so fascinated and diverted by the media histrionics of the powerful that we may downplay considerations of legitimacy and interest. We may find a North amusing as a folkish hero, forgetting his defiance of legitimate authority; we may find a Reagan attractive playing President, and suppress awareness that it might not be in our economic interest to accord him power. When politics becomes play, opinion may seek and find folktales that outweigh all other considerations. The charm of an avuncular Reagan and the instant charisma of a North may be sweet cheats of folkish entertainment, but one can be swept away in the celebration of a folkish hero and the patriotic fervor he or she can elicit through the dramatization of folk identity. We might remind ourselves of what the great German writer Thomas Mann said of Nazism: "National Socialism means: 'I do not care for the social issue. What I want is the folk tale'."[12]

The Captivity Narrative

The captivity narrative is a popularly-derived story that has deep indigenous roots in American history, particularly with our frontier experience and the development of the mythology of a free people. Since we thought of ourselves as a people who had just been freed from foreign bondage, yet faced the hostility of an unknown continent and native aborigines, we began to develop a narrative tradition about threats to our freedom from both foreign and domestic aliens. The tales of women and children kidnapped by the Indians date from Puritan times, beginning a popular story formula that has taken on many different forms (e.g., children taken by wandering Gypsies). Such tales often had psychosexual roots, involving fantasies about the sexual prowess of savages unrepressed by Christian civilization. In any case, they fed social suspicions about the motives of those stigmatized as "unAmerican," who for racial or ethnic reasons were not deemed part of the new community. The captivity narrative would undergird political policies and actions, justifying hostile actions against threats to the expanding United States. The political relevance of the captivity narrative resides in the persistent power of the story, supporting the general sense that the worst fate for Americans is to be held captive, either physically or mentally, by an alien force. This narrative tradition usually had a climactic rescue such as the U.S. Cavalry rescuing settlers held by the Indians which not only saved the hostages from an unspeakable fate but punished the evil aliens. With the emergence of forms of mass mediation—the dime novel, magazines and newspapers, the movies, radio and television—the captivity narrative would find all sorts of formulations in ever new settings.

The ancient folktale of captivity, then, affects popular expectations about the world, and thereby the political importance accorded hostage situations. In this way, what people perceive as important in politics may be derived from a widespread folktale, one that is forever revalidated in importance by fresh retellings. A popular narrative then becomes an integral part of the political culture, a subtle consideration in the exercise of power. If so, our popular desire for dramatic resolution of captivity narratives becomes an expectation then transferred to politics. The Presidencies of both Carter and Reagan were adversely affected by their understanding of the importance of hostage resolution, through their attempts to resolve hostage situations in which Americans were being held against their will. Carter was defeated in 1980 in part because of the Iranian hostage stalemate, but Reagan, who came into office vowing no more hostage deals, was himself embroiled in a politically embarrassing and debilitating scandal stemming from the effort to ransom a few Americans held in Lebanon. Reagan's invasion of Grenada was justified in terms of his determination to avoid a hostage crisis, given media celebration with the sight of American students kissing native soil on their return (although apparently they were never in danger). Too, the captivity folktale also affects policy, even though there may be scant evidence of actual capture. In recent years, the captivity story persisted in two major and politically-charged forms: the foreign fantasy of hordes of MIA's (missing in action) held captive in Indochina, and the domestic fantasy of great numbers of children kidnapped by alien forces (cults, slavers, pedophiles, etc.). There was much symbolic political effort expended assuring MIA families and the public that the government was doing everything possible to find and free the (likely non-existent) MIA's in southeast Asia. Too, a great deal of domestic effort was devoted to the fantasy of children being abducted by evil strangers, although statistics clearly indicated that most "missing" children were runaways or taken by one parent from another in a disintegrating family, and that only a minuscule number were taken forcibly by strangers. However, the power of the captivity narrative is such that much rhetorical energy was expended expressing political concern, and a network of public and private organizations publicized missing children as a national crisis. The faces of the missing were posted everywhere, including on milk cartons; made for TV specials and movies (ranging from the many films based on the classic Western captivity tale, *The Searchers*, to *Aliens*); parents fingerprinted and videotaped their children in case of abduction, and a few even put identification microdots in their children's molars; an entire how-to-protect-your-children industry appeared, with books, lectures, and training programs; a national 800-number missing-children hotline was established; and Congress declared a National Missing Children's Day and held hearings featuring testimony about Satanic cults kidnapping children for sacrifices.

The captivity narrative is a clear example of how recurrent habits of popular thought, emergent in a present as play, can affect the conduct of politics, at least in terms of symbolic reassurance that produces quiescence. Deeply rooted popular folklore does constitute a habit, in the sense of a mythic resource that reappears in ever new form but retells an old, old story. The great fund of popular folklore a culture perpetuates is an integral, if subtle and oblique, part of the political folkways that give politics its distinctive—and to the uninitiated, puzzling—flavor. But unless the "habits of the heart" of Americans are severely torn asunder, talks such as the captivity narrative will continue to appear as a form of popular play, and a folktale that calls for political response.[13]

Popular Political Talk

Before the days of systematic polling, one of the common ways for politicians and journalists to get some idea of what was on people's minds was to make a tour of an area talking to the "barber-shop crowd." The fellows who sat around neighborhood or small town barbershops engaged in popular talk, including talk about politics. By finding out what these locals were talking about, one could "feel the pulse" of the public. Such informal political inquiry was an astute recognition that much political perception and attitude has its genesis in such talk. In such settings, popular knowledge—the languages of the folk—finds a wide variety of expression, some of which people use for its political application. An individual or a group may apply criteria of evaluation to an event or process that political elites find uninformed and wrongheaded, but that doesn't affect a popular idea's potency. For example, during gas shortages politicians and economists can explain the political and economic exigencies that bring about shortages and price rises, but popular talk may come up with a very different explanation: gas shortages are a hoax and excuse used by oil companies to raise prices. Such a widespread popular explanation may not be based in fact or drawn from an authoritative source, but is given credence by some popular authority (a relative or friend, for instance) or through group validation (everyone in the barbershop agrees that gas prices are manipulated). Such immediate explanations may have roots in myth and legend (conspiracy theories), but they are a response to current events that gives them some kind of understandable and expressible meaning.

One of the more astonishing forms of popular expression attributing meaning is the habit of according immortality to great heroes and villains. This is rooted in the recurrent desire to believe that such figures have divine or demonic mantles that make them transcend death. Throughout history, popular legends have persisted that great heroes still live and will some day return. The obvious figure that comes to mind is King Arthur, but the same folktale has arisen around figures such as Alexander the Great, Charlemagne, and Emiliano Zapata. More recently, tales have persisted about popular heroes who suddenly die in youth—James Dean, Jim Morrison, and Elvis Presley—who are still alive. "Elvis sightings" became a common folk tale with recurrent outbreaks around his birthdate, date of death, or birth of grandchildren. But undoubtedly the most persistent story is the tale that John F. Kennedy is alive, having somehow survived the assassination in 1963. Kennedy has been variously known to be still in the hospital in Dallas, on the top floor of Bethesda Naval Hospital, on a Greek island owned by Aristotle Onassis, and so on. Word-of-mouth evidence always comes from someone who knows someone who knows someone, and so on. Such views are much supported by the various weekly tabloids, who survive and prosper in part because of their feel for discovering and perpetuating such stories. The same sort of process works with persistent stories of the survival of great evildoers. Jim Jones did not meet his demise with his flock at Jonestown, the story goes, but rather escaped and lurks somewhere out there in the jungle. The most popular of all villains, Adolf Hitler, has recurrently been reported alive since 1945, a tabloid story that persists because of people's desire to believe in the indestructibility of evil, and perhaps in some cases even because of a latent admiration of a "mad and evil genius" with such hypnotic and destructive powers. In any case, on the occasion of his one hundredth birthdate, tabloids were still carrying the tale of the great dictator alive in some obscure place, awaiting no doubt his moment to return to a renascent and unified Germany.[14] Many of the people who are drawn to or love to tell such folktales are often "inside-dopesters," people who enjoy communicating to others what is *really* happening, what undercurrent is going on, who is really in charge, what is certain to happen. Knowing the inside-dope makes someone feel knowledgeable, possessing privileged information that everyone else ignorant of, since they do not have access to the true sources of popular knowledge. Perhaps the most pervasive inside-dope stories that recurs, taking on different form for new exigencies with various groups, is the conspiracy theory. Theories of conspiracy have persisted as both an elite and popular folktale from time immemorial, with various candidates for the conspiratorial group that is actually behind everything—Satan and his minions, the international Jewish conspiracy, the Knights Templar, the Masonic order, the international banking cabal, the Trilateral Commission, and so on endlessly. Evangelical Christians who were part of the New Right discovered secular humanists, alleged to be the conspiracy in charge of government, education, and other institutions, and bent on undermining Christian (or at least one definition of Christianity) civilization. If people feel powerless, sensing that they are left out of the symbolic and material fruits of power, then there is a temptation to believe that the powerful are conspiring to destroy them. After a decade of being decidedly left out of power, American blacks began in the early 1990s to talk about "The Plan," a conspiracy theory that circulated the streets of inner city ghettos. The Plan, so went the story, was the concerted and secret effort by the white Establishment to destroy all forms of black power by discrediting or jailing black leaders, and using drugs, alcohol, cigarettes, AIDS, and so on to commit black genocide. Like all other conspiracy theories, there was scant evidence that such a conspiracy was creating such havoc, but the plain proof of the decline of black life and the general sense of powerlessness made many people listen to tales of The Plan. The inside dope may be incorrect, but if it is validated by word-of-mouth in streets, churches, and barber shops, then it takes on the explosive quality of being believed, with the hidden enemy of the people now unmasked for what it is.[15]

Popular talk that has the political relevance may take on a wide variety of forms. When some political story is told, say about corruption, this may occasion the utterance of a folk proverb drawn from the apocrypha of barber shop wisdom to the effect that all politicians are crooks. Prejudices not only against politicians but against any stigmatized group is activated in such talk, with slights against the hated group—blacks, Jews, women, you name it—made legitimate to say, since the group apparently shares them (dissenting in a highly prejudicial group is difficult and even dangerous). Prejudicial views, or for that matter any kind of view, tend to become stronger and more "reinforced" when they are consensually validated in a group. Most of the time such negative views of a stigmatized "out-group" are just idle talk that serves nothing more than the group purpose of feeling superior and smug. But group consensus on outsiders can lead to feelings of inner strength and outer threat, leading to a sense of vulnerability and willingness to use violence. Such feelings likely precede many group attacks on racial outsiders, a recurrent problem in a racially and ethnically diverse society.

Every new social and political cleavage will inspire popular talk about the dangers of possibilities of innovation, and what kind of folk responses are feasible. The feminist movement brought about jokes about women among male groups, usually with a decidedly anti-feminist flavor. There have long been jokes about homosexuals, but the AIDS epidemic occasioned a whole genre of "cruelty jokes" about the "gay disease" and prominent homosexuals such as Rock Hudson. Even traumatic events with loss of life, such as the Challenger and Chernobyl accidents, bring about the telling of widely circulated and virtually immediate jokes about the event. Such jokes are often prejudicial and cruel, but serve the function of relieving tension about a process or event. Humor also can be used to satirize the pretensions of politicians, especially when they get themselves in great political trouble. When Gary Hart's extramarital exploits were revealed, his political reputation was at least temporarily destroyed, partially through the many jokes that circulated about his indiscretions, labeling him as a fool rather than a hero. Like other forms of popular expression, jokes communicate to a group some definition of a political situation, placing something in a humorous—and often lewd and irreverent— context. At their best, they remind folks of the human, and political, comedy, and inform those that share the laugh on how to think about the larger world of change and stress.

We are now close to what we might call the social unspoken. In popular talk, oftentimes there are taboos on certain subjects, especially, as we say, in "mixed company." But many people may have ideas or images they do not speak about with others but which they still privately entertain. People may have dark sexual desires they do not overtly express, but which they covertly fantasize about. Or they may secretly wish that a despised politician would be assassinated, but make a publicly acceptable statement that assassination is a bad thing. The realm of the *political unspoken* now may include the many people who still secretly hold racial and sexual prejudices but do not speak about them, except in secret ways. (There is often a disparity between the people who say to pollsters that they are going to vote for a black or woman candidate for office, and those who actually do, voting in secret). In the realm of the socially unexpressed, we are dealing with our popular talk with ourselves, latent thoughts which are often forbidden from social enunciation but which we hold to as part of our secret subjective life. Since such unspoken thoughts are suppressed, understanding how widespread and how important these latent feelings are for politics can only be inferred from indirect clues.

If something cannot be expressed openly in polite society, people find ways to experience a covert, or latent culture, that gives secret voice to their private thoughts. But if we examine what it is that people read, watch, listen to, and so on, we get some notion of a popular undercurrent with potential political relevance. Such activity is in a sense popular talk with an auditor with whom one communicates interests and desires that are not expressible in "respectable" circles. Here, though, the communication is surreptitious and often unrespectable. A pillar of the church and community in a small town might enjoy a secret life quietly buying and reading salacious pornography, feeding secret fantasies about sexual ecstasy and even perversion unknown to his or her family and friends. It is common for families to discover after their death that the loved one had a "secret life" of which they knew nothing, since the departed had been able to keep the covert world which she or he disappeared into a private secret.

But it is those widespread guilty pleasures that might have some political relevance in that they reveal an attitudinal tip of a submerged iceberg. If significant segments of the populace engage in some form of slightly disreputable or disguised activity, then we perhaps are glimpsing the underside of people's overt and sanctioned face to the world. Let us take the example of the feminist movement, which has had significant effect on American society over the past several decades. Despite many setbacks (ERA) and controversies (abortion), feminism has had both a rhetorical and policy influence, even among conservatives. Republican administrations feel compelled to include women in high positions, and to acquiesce in acceptance of many feminist principles (suppressing sexist talk, treating women workers fairly, and so on). But we may wonder whether the success of feminism has not driven more archaic and even primal feelings into covert forms of expression. Both women and men may feel more constrained as to what they can openly express about sexual experience, so they find modes of expression in a variety of disreputable forms—women-in-chains movies, pornography, treks to clubs featuring male or female erotic dancers, or dirty jokes. Slightly more reputable, and certainly widespread, are popular novels. American women consume enormous numbers of "romance" novels, although many of them are more erotical than romantic. Although the Harlequin romance novels keep their heroines virginal, most of the others do not, pacing their heroines through a wide variety of peak sexual experiences. The popularity of such novels in the decades since the feminist movement began suggests a possible link. Not only do such novels let women fantasize about adventure, romance, and erotic experience denied them in ordinary life, they also allow them a private fantasy about a direct and primal relationship between a strong and sensual man uncomplicated by the social innovations of feminism. How much such a submerged life affects, for example, voting will always remain unclear, yet romance novels do seem to reveal feelings that in political terms are anti-feminist and reactionary.

Even more astonishing are the male-oriented fantasy novels that envision an alternative world which reasserts the "proper" relationship between men and women. The widely read *Gor* novels (at last count, there were twenty-five or so of them) are a Nietzchean fantasy about a primitive Dark Age planet of male warriors and heroic adventures. But the Goreans are more than just a sword-and-sorcerer world; they are primarily a place in which women are subjugated into abject slavery, which through punishment and degradation at the hands of powerful warrior-men they learn to love as their true natural state. Beautiful and assertive feminist-women are kidnapped from Earth, a hellish place because of the emasculation of men through female equality; but on Gor, women achieve renewed sensual pride as total slaves of dominant men, and men revivify their natural masculine essence through the conquest of women. Such a popular formula suggests a fantasy of a kind of archaic fascism based on the power of a dominant sex to subordinate, and elicit enthusiastic obedience from, another. The Gor novels and related popular fare posit an unspoken sadomasochistic basis for male-female relations that run squarely against the spoken rhetorical consensus on mutual treatment. But if such popular novels are any indication, just beneath the surface there is considerable play with the idea of an alternative world of female bondage-and-discipline, raw male sexual power, and the restoration of women to some sort of primal state of obedient sensuality and slave mentality. As with the romance novels, we are in the realm of unspoken desires with unknown political relevance, but both suggest a submerged dissatisfaction with the contemporary sexual ethos that if channeled into political energy could disrupt the rhetorical and social arrangement of power between the sexes.

Conclusion

We have here claimed that the flow of popular discourse is at the base of popular culture. If people in contemporary society decide what's happening on the basis of popular knowledge, then it follows that we are in the realm of contemporary popular folklore. By translating talk into stories, the folk perpetuate understanding of the world in which they live. At the ill-understood base of politics is this popular universe of discourse, a world that expands the realm of folklore into the study of contemporary political folklore. Like the anthropologists who study teenage culture and corporate rituals, folklorists who seek popular knowledge about politics and society should boldly go where no folklorist has gone before, into barber shops, bars, and health clubs in search of the popular mind.

Chapter Three
Heroic Stories and American Politics:
Myths of Adventure, Romance, and Mystery

We have argued that the "flow of popular discourse" in popular life is the folkish basis of popular culture, however it may be exploited and channeled by elites, ranging from the writers of popular books to the producers of popular television. As comparative mythologists and folklorists have long tried to demonstrate, there are familiar patterns to popular stories that seem to transcend time and place, as well as elite control. At the core of world wide popular storytelling are myths of the hero. Since almost every culture has some sort of conception of "cultural heroism," popular stories circulate over space and propagate over time the value of such heroic character and action. Heroic tales are often the centerpiece of mythologies, assuring a culture of the efficacy of heroic action in a mythic time in the past or future, and offering the hero as a valid icon usable for action in a present. When we see recurrent and recognizable stories appearing in bookstands and on television that can be traced back for generations, then we are observing a mythic narrative with cultural and political resilience.

In the United States, the overarching "myth of the State" is usually referred to as "the American Dream." Such a vague but persistent idea usually centers on the shimmering prospect of the destined completion of individual and national goals through the enactment of heroic roles and the achievement of shared values. The myth of the American dream is in politics a powerful rhetorical and propaganda theme, a mythic reference that frames debates between conservatives and liberals as to what policies will best realize the completion of the dream. Although different ideological positions will disagree on collective policy, there is in the American political culture a very strong strain that defines the completion

45

of the dream as an individual enterprise. This is a mythic constraint, since in fact much "individual achievement" that shapes the individualistic rhetoric of established and wealthy elites was sponsored by mercantile alliances with government (railroad development, the defense industry, and so on) and government projects such as warfare and space exploration. Individualism is thereby used as a symbol that defends inequality be perpetuating the myth that achievement is earned, and that those who have wealth and power (and those who don't) deserve their station in life. Yet the myth of the individual realization of the Dream is widely held among the populace, even though there is widespread programatic support for collective measures such as national health care that makes individual health a matter of public policy. This contradiction, however, does not appear to lessen our desire for mythic vindication by telling ourselves stories about, and admiring, heroes who exemplify virtues we associate with individualism—pluck, courage, cunning, physical prowess, rectitude, a charismatic aura, a sense that the hero is lucky. Like every other culture, we mix up fictional and real conceptions of the heroic, adapting them to changing circumstances from both our narrative and historical experience, giving us a stock of heroes and heroic virtues we may use for our own purposes.

The authors of *Habits of the Heart* make a worthwhile distinction between "utilitarian individualism" and "expressive individualism."[1] Utilitarian individualism we may take to be the mythic heroism that drives the economy, featuring the utility of individual achievement through work that creates prosperity. Expressive individualism we infer to be the heroism of culture that drives enterprises such as the consumer culture and leisure activities, feature the legitimate expression of individual achievement through play. But they do not talk about what we might call "civic individualism," the mythic heroism that drives politics, featuring individual achievement through political entrepreneurship. Those individuals who achieve in all three areas of endeavor are following the bliss of mythic heroism, and become the object of both cultural honor and criticism. The individual who acquires great wealth will be honored as a social beneficiary and damned as a "robber baron" or "corporate raider." Heroes of leisure can include exemplary figures offered as a model for youth to emulate (Lou Gehrig, Michael Jordan), or condemned as a threat to morals (Elvis Presley, Hugh

Hefner). Political heroes may range from those seen as national heroes (Andrew Jackson) or civic reformers (Martin Luther King, Jr.) on the one hand, to politically fearsome (John Brown) or loathsome (Richard Nixon) leaders. All forms of achievement can lead to a status of either heroism or villainy or foolery, depending on reputation and timing. The beneficent "captains of industry" of the Coolidge prosperity of the 1920s became the malevolent "economic royalists" of the Depression. In any case, politics is a forum for heroic action, and we see this as a matter of individual achievement: figures such as Jackson or Lincoln or Reagan are the beneficiaries of their own talents and ambitions, we believe, and are celebrated as personages just as deserving of our praise as those who became rich or famous. In this sense, we see politics as a major stage for dramas of the American monomyth.

The American political monomyth is a variant of the process (discussed in the classic work by Jewett and Lawrence) by which the individual hero acts for and redeems the community.[2] We are no less immune than other peoples from the hope that only a hero can save us, since we cannot save ourselves. The myth of economic individualism gives legitimacy to the unequal accumulation of wealth; the myth of cultural individualism gives legitimacy to the unequal accumulation of cultural objects such as art or fame; and the myth of political individualism gives legitimacy to the unequal accumulation of power. The monomyth suggests that the many have no right to block the path to glory of the one. There are many counterbalances to such individual endeavor, but the persistence of the myth may make us wonder if Americans believe more in accumulative rather than distributive justice. Further, reliance on or acquiescence in the redemptive powers of a hero acting alone is patently undemocratic, justifying not only highly concentrated power but also limited responsibility on the part of the heroic actor to the community. If the hero comes to believe that his or her accumulation of wealth is justified by individual merit and not social leadership, then any sense of philanthropic or communitarian responsibility may be missing. Thus a corporate leader may destroy a city dependent upon that corporation for pure profit without any sense of guilt; private investors may bid up art without any feeling that art belongs to the artistic community; and politicians may aggrandize power through manipulatory politics that violate civilized norms of the political community without seeing the harm that does to the people they lead and betray. But in all cases, the myth of individualism remains so powerful that we tolerate its consequences, and recurrently hold out hope for its renewed efficacy to save us from ourselves.

The heroic myth in the United States has powerful antecedents that continue to perpetuate it through popular culture. Here we wish to discuss it using John Cawelti's familiar distinction between adventure, mystery, and romance. But we want to extend his analysis by using those categories (which, admittedly, intermingle) as a framework for three major antecedents of popular heroism with political relevance: the Western adventure, the domestic romance, and the urban mystery. The Western hero is a cultural exemplar of the power of conquest; the romantic hero represents the power of social adjustment; and the urban hero exemplifies the power of survival. We will discuss them in turn. Then we will look at the question of female heroism, since these myths have largely been the province of male heroics.

The Western Epic

Students of the popular mind are well aware of the conflict between academic and critical history over popular history. The popular belief in the American Dream has over generations been enshrined in the patriotic symbols of the republic as manifest in historic events and personages—the Revolution, the Civil War, the Great Presidents. In the popular past, national history comes to be celebrated as a patriotic pageant, often suppressing the ugly and evil and emphasizing instead symbols of national pride. When critical historians intent on breaking icons cast doubt on, say, the unblemished character of George Washington, the purity of motives of the signers of the constitution, or the humane nature of the war against Japan, then they can be accused of being unpatriotic for not espousing the "kind of history" that should be taught the schoolchildren. Patriotic history obviously serves the purposes of state propaganda and popular reassurance of national worth, putting pressure on schools to perpetuate shared mythology. It is likely that one of the great sources of political reactionary movements, such as the one led by Reagan, aims at the restoration of a sense of national worth and progress by insisting on the veracity of mythic history and the misguided or unpatriotic nature of the historical iconoclasts. In a sense, such struggles are over whether national history is sacred or profane. If the past is sacred, then it is beyond criticism and should be venerated for its moral and political instruction; if the past is profane, then it is beneath veneration and should be criticized.

This is nowhere more evident than in our attitude toward our great national epic, the winning of the West. The Western drama is central to our mythic heritage, and indeed is likely our greatest contribution to the mythic legacy we will leave the world. The Western story is actually a substory of the larger myth of the New World and its promise of renewal for humankind. Indeed, the entire settlement of North America is a story of the movement of a new civilization west into the wilderness, creating the mythic dynamic of what Frederick Jackson Turner called "the meeting point between savagery and civilization." It was this conflict between the "new man," the American, and what the unknown wilderness held that gave the Western narrative its power. For sacralized patriotic history, the winning of the West constituted an epic folktale of national character and destiny, forming the geopolitical basis for "the last best hope of mankind," the United States. The Western epic was a conquest, a triumph of determined individualism by democratic heroes—trailblazers, mountain men, cattlemen, sodbusters, gamblers, gunfighters, goldseekers, madonnas of the plains and prostitutes—all of whom exemplify the American Dream's tenet that one can seek a new start in a new country that welcomes initiative and daring. The story of the West was violent but redemptive, and thus by creating this new civilization made the epic trek one worth celebrating in story and song.[3]

For others, however, the myth of the West is just myth in the sense of a false belief. The critical mind looks at the West and sees profane history now enshrined in national popular fare. The conquest of the continent was an epic of environmental and aboriginal destruction that was violent but not redemptive, since the primary motive was plunder. What has been enshrined in popular culture and uncritical history books is a justification for exploitation, violent struggles over property, and virtual genocide of the native American. Nor was the settling of the West even a forum for the exercise of individualism, since much of what happened was the collective effort of groups acting in concert rather than the product of the efforts of a lone individual. There was nothing particularly self-reliant or ingenious about the pioneers,

and they would have been astonished that they had been elevated
to such an heroic status. But worst of all, the myth of the West
perpetuates some of the less admirable traits among Americans:
their penchant for violence, the ubiquity of guns in an urbanized
world, their attraction to political figures who exploit the simplistic
shoot-it-out ethos of the Western in an age of nuclear weapons.
In this view, the Western myth is not only historically inaccurate
and misleading, it is downright dangerous, threatening to make
the United States into an outlaw nation with a reputation for
resorting to violence to bully its way but remaining outside of the
civilized family of nations. From this view, the nation has become
both a prisoner and victim of its own popular mythology, unable
to face up to or deal realistically with an outside world that doesn't
share our vision of "manifest destiny," a kind of national
individualism gone mad.

It remains to be seen how much we are truly going to be bound
by the "culturo-logic" of the Western myth. But its power and
persistence cannot be denied, nor the fact that it retains enormous
political significance. The critical historians may be strictly correct
that the West is a fiction, but it is through such mythic fictions
that many of us understand the world, and wish the world to live
up to the expectations derived from our most venerable and trusted
story forms. At the very core of the Western formula is a folktale
of raw democratic justice done in a savage and hostile world. The
many versions of fictional drama that originally comprised the
Western pitted the American against forces with whom he struggled
and triumphed, representing a just triumph of democratic man
against dark forces of nature. Every time the Indians or outlaws
or simply the frontier were defeated, it demonstrated the power
of American conquest. Individual heroes were part of a grand heroic
march towards the conquest of our manifest destiny, the teleological
end of our redemptive task as a nation. Since civilization was
advanced by such conquest, this justified independent and private
violent action in pursuit of individual goals. Individualism thereby
became the catalyst for the creation of a virtuous order, perpetuating
the idea that American civilization is ultimately based on violence.

The dramatic logic of the Western myth is imbedded deeply
in the national mind, persisting down to the present. The West
has always been a "country of the mind," a concept as much as
a place, fundamental to our optimistic hopes of the realization of

the drama of democracy. It can be argued that the Western story is our most fundamental popular adventure. Beginning with the first accounts of exploration, Puritan tales of captivity, down to Leatherstocking, the dime novel, Wild West shows and rodeos, and perhaps most of all the movies, the Western became an integral part of our fictional stock and a subtle force on our political perspective and self-image. The Western myth is also extremely flexible, allowing for a wide variety of story formulas, heroes, and plots that change over time, representing changing attitudes and concerns. Practically any social problem—racism, sexism, war, exploitation—can be presented as something that was soluble through heroic action occurring in the symbolic landscape of our mythic time and place. However, that landscape is also a political geography, since it presents a primal scene for how contemporary problems can be addressed as they might have been in our collective country of the mind. The myth of the West thereby acquires a measure of dramatic adequacy, urging on us the question of how we can make the contemporary world live up to the standards of the mythic world. Why indeed doesn't the cavalry come in time?

It was noted at the time of the Iran hostage crisis in 1979-80 that we wanted "cinemaphotogenic solutions" where the cavalry did come in time to rescue American held in captivity.[4] The fact that we did try an "air cavalry" rescue in Iran, and failing that, heeded and elected as President a politician who had long been steeped in the mythography of Hollywood and advocated heroic intervention. Reagan's own intervention in Grenada in 1983, and his successor Bush's in Panama in 1989, was couched in the rhetoric of justifiable heroic action led by the President-cavalryman. The Western myth had stigmatized enemies on both frontiers as threatening barbarians who had to be resisted and punished through heroic action. Today hostile leaders and forces in Third World countries are cast as the barbarians who must be found by a righteous force. Such military actions have the Western myth of heroic intervention as a referent and metaphor, providing a ground of mythic justification for the use of the military as a punitive force against "barbarian" threats. American military adventures now occur on new frontiers and with new savages to fight.

In his excellent work on American myth and Vietnam, John Hellmann examines the extent to which the Western myth was interwoven with our heroic intervention in Indochina. The Green

Beret soldier, for example, adopted in story and song the iconography of the frontier hero, possessing the virtues of both the civilization from which they came and the jungle wilderness that they would conquer. Such inheritors of the mantle of the hardy frontier hero would "perform a symbolic drama of America's remembered past and dreamed future." By fighting on such a new frontier, we would again achieve the heroic virtue of regeneration through violence. Later on, the mythic pattern is disturbed when we realized the adventure had become a nightmare, shattering our faith in the mythic adequacy of the Western story to guide us in the pursuit of adventurous quests. Military actions such as Grenada or Panama in this light are not so much adventures as military theatrics that give media display to Presidential bravado, suggesting a desperate hope on the part of both political elites and part of the public that we might in the post-Vietnam world regain something of the Western spirit.[5]

It was indeed during the wake of the Vietnam experience that the Western began to undergo basic transformation as a mythic drama. It became less a heroic morality play and more a forum for criticism of American heroic motives and society. It is true that such criticisms had existed before, as in the social consciousness of *The Ox-Bow Incident* or the demonic underside of heroism as revealed by the Wayne characters in *Red River* and *The Searchers*. But with films like *Little Big Man*, much of the traditional Western formula was inverted, and heroes such as Eastwood or Bronson acquired a more violent and self-serving mystique. The later Wayne movies (*Chisum* and *Big Jake*) show him as a kind of Western Godfather-Protector who should be obeyed to protect us from an Hobbesian world, much like the argument made by the Nixon White House. His final film, *The Shootist*, ends with the Western hero simply shooting it out with invited enemies for no community purpose and for no moral point, violence for violence's sake. Western novels such as the Longarm series featured heroes who were paragons of sexual and violent prowess, but offered little else that was admirable or beneficial. Other Westerns concentrated on the Professional, the individuals and groups who were supremely competent but committed only to technique, much like the political consultants of today who run campaigns and make slick propaganda for whomever pays them, or astronauts who parley professional skill into political careers.

It has even been suggested that the Western myth has now become not only obsolete but downright pernicious. A figure of popular culture such as J.R. Ewing of TV's *Dallas* becomes both a parody and perversion of the Western myth, a Sunbelt entrepreneur exploring the new frontiers of sexual and environmental exploitation, pure greed, and political nihilism. As President, Ronald Reagan affected the manner and trappings of the Westerner, with his "ranch in the sky," horseback riding, and designer Western clothes, as well as his aw-shucks but tough-talking swagger. Janice Hocker Rushing referred to this as "pseudo-synthesis" of the archetypical heroic image, glossing over the contradictions and dangers of such a pretense in the nuclear and corporate age. Yet this transforms the Western hero into a political "pseudo-event" wherein one plays at the appearance of fulfilling the myth while actually not doing so. But ultimately that makes many suspect that the Western myth is an act and sham, and is ultimately subversive of the myth.[6] George Bush also tried to identify with the Western myth, affecting ten-gallon hats and his connection with Texas, but that was counterpoised with his elite Establishment ties and "preppy" manner.

In any case, the Western as a form of popular entertainment lingers on, but in some media, such as the movies and television, it is severely marginalized. But if it is the case that the Western is our basic story of adventure, then the myth may be now undergoing transformation, transcending its traditional social and political use and discovering new frontiers of adventure. In the past, the Western was a justification for righteous empire backed by violent enforcement. Perhaps in the future there will be other frontiers, and different definitions of what constitutes a frontier into which we might venture. Space is obviously the "final frontier" into which we might venture, yet we have not fully adopted a new myth that would lead us to seek the enlightenment envisioned by, say, Kubrick's film *2001*. Many have interpreted the *Star Wars* trilogy as a new myth, but others see Lucas' films as some very old myth— the American Adam using violence in a new wilderness in defense of righteous empire—given renewed justification. In the "warriors of the wasteland" movies (*Road Warrior*), the futuristic post-apocalyptic setting is tamed from new barbarians in the guise of Dark Age warriors by a Western-like hero who defeats such tribes for the nascent primitive but peaceable community attempting to re-establish civilization. Other forms of adventure in the Western tradition that have emerged recently include the "return to Vietnam" fantasy, rescuing hostages and wreaking revenge on the barbarians who defeated us, or intervening in other fantastic settings (as in the Rambo films). Too, the space Western can include mythic opportunities for women as agents of vengeance, as in the "Rambolina" film *Aliens*.

Perhaps most promising is for the Western myth to turn from the redemption of the American scene through violent heroic action to one that redeems the scene through transforming our symbolic landscape into the Garden of the World. Complementing the Western myth of heroic drama was the transformation of the land from a place of confrontation and strife into a peaceable kingdom in harmony with nature. In an older image, the Western adventure made the world safe for exploitation, since the civilization created was one of unlimited prosperity. But this did violence to the environment, and decades of exploitation and expansion now does threaten the purity of the Garden. Perhaps in the future some visionary politician will appeal to the spirit of Western Adventure for the restoration of the land in accordance with the pastoral Dream of America as a unspoiled Eden. The American Dream would then be a drama of scenic purification, not of barbarians and aliens that must be expunged through the violent action of an heroic agent, but through concerted community effort that acts upon the myth of the American West in an epic effort to remake the country once again into a virgin land.

The Romantic Hero

In its classic formulation, the Western hero served the function of advancing the outer limits of civilization. Today those who are identified as "cowboys"—astronauts, truck drivers, Sunbelt entrepreneurs, and politicians seeking a macho image—are less agents who exercise power on behalf of the community and more a favored few who have managed to acquire the means to escape ordinary life. Those who can go into space or hit the open road in their truck or fly about in their jets have transcended the bounds of earth and the responsibilities of community leadership. Even Presidents (especially since Reagan) seem now to have acquired a status of popular hero with the power of conquering limits on self-expression, but with self-imposed limits ("nothing can be done") on the power of conquering social problems. Like the Westerner, such figures roam but do not settle, flaunt their independent inner-direction rather than their socially responsible other-direction. The paradox actually was always there in the Western hero: he was usually someone who acted for the community but was not of it, a model of self-reliance whose power derived from his independence. Once the trouble that beset the community was resolved, he had to leave, since his social function had been exhausted. In its current corrupted state, the ethos of the Western hero appears to be independent even of that, as someone (such as the contemporary superrich) whose power to wander includes contempt for the common life.

In both traditional and contemporary heroism, then, this means that social leadership of the common life is the province of what we will term the romantic hero. In fact, we exclude various kinds of romantic heroes—swashbucklers, mad geniuses, for instance—who are agents of adventure. What is of political interest is the heroic image of the domestic male leader, someone who does accept responsibility for what happens to the settled democratic community. His power is not conquest through violence, but rather peacemaking through social negotiation. He is not independent nor inner-directed, but rather dependent and other-directed. His task is not the establishment of a community, nor its defense from external threats, but rather its continuation as a place that fulfills the promise of the American Dream. He wants to advance the inner limits of civilization by making the community live up to its values, appealing to the emotional bonds of community which transcend individualism. The domestic romantic is no loner, outsider, or wanderer; he is destined to be the gregarious center of family, friends, and society, a creature not of the territory outside but the society inside the town. His power lies in giving society direction, and his method is persuasion, not force. His leadership stems from being a nice guy, one of the fellows, a regular, someone who is thoroughly domesticated and housebroken, without guile or spite, an ordinary man safe at home in our town.

Rather than the extraordinary Westerner armed with his power of conquest, it is the ordinary townsman who is the "natural" leader of society. The Westerner has uses (as in 1980 with Reagan's bravado) when the political community feels besieged. But when people seek domestic tranquility, a government with which they feel comfortable, a social leader with familiar and ordinary traits is preferable. In mythic terms, the townsman-leader is likely a descendant of the peaceful yoeman farmer whose stalwart labor created the Garden of the World. In the post-World War II period, the townsman became the core male power of the affluent bourgeois society, presiding over the expanse of suburban life. His immediate domains are the world of work as dominant utilitarian individual, and world of expressive play centered on the nuclear family in the modal single dwelling. His social benevolence and wisdom were celebrated in such forums as 1950s TV family comedies, as well as his comic temperament. His essential character is that of a romantic conservative, sentimentally attached to the institutions and habits of the social order, and committed to the emotional health of the town. He wishes to live out the romance of American normalcy, the monomyth of freedom in conformity, redemption through the peaceful pursuit of happiness.

In a broad sense, we might say that the Western hero represents the ideal of freedom, while the Town hero represents the ideal of virtue. The Westerner is free from society, so his virtue stems from his freedom; the Townsman is in society, so his freedom stems from his virtue. The Westerner is free to adventure in a world beyond normalcy; the Townsman is free to develop his virtue in the romance of normalcy. We may illustrate these differently, but often complementary, conceptions of male heroism by reference to two major icons that exemplify them: John Wayne and James Stewart. The Wayne of his greatest Western films (*Stagecoach, She Wore A Yellow Ribbon, Red River, The Searchers, The Man Who Shot Liberty Valance, The Shootist*) is a man of violence who freely moves on the fringes of society, but whose true milieu is "the wild country." He exemplifies the anarchic freedom—and loneliness— of the true Westerner, forever separated from society and destined to never be part of anything beyond nature. But contrast him with the vintage Stewart character (*Mr. Smith Goes to Washington, It's a Wonderful Life, Harvey*), a happy romantic who exemplifies the benefits of local involvement. "George Bailey" of *It's a Wonderful Life* is both of and in Bedford Falls, and discovers that he is essential to maintaining its essential goodness from internal threats. The circle of family and friends that support him in crisis demonstrates the power of social leadership to sustain such a "midworld." Stewart, unlike Wayne, is the quintessential "average man," the individual in the mass who makes his mark by not standing out. His domestic credentials make him a local leader by being so thoroughly enfolded in the community.

In politics, would-be leaders contesting in elections or otherwise vying for power attempt to appeal to both heroic traditions, emphasizing one or the other depending upon the mood of the public. Ronald Reagan attempted to combine both, self-casting himself as a Wayne-like advocate of Western values and solutions, complemented by his Stewart-like air of nice-guy social leadership and family commitment. His successor Bush attempted the same combination, combating his "wimp" image by self-portrayal as a Westerner who identified with the "cult of toughness," but also as a kind and gentle grandfather presiding over an extended family. By creating an image of both a bold adventurer and domestic romantic, such media politicians exploit deeply rooted heroic traditions, combining them for political communication if not for political action. The brief invasions of both Grenada and Panama may be viewed as attempts to "prove" their adherence to the code of the West, and their elaborate attempts to publicly demonstrate their social gregariousness and ordinariness shows awareness of the importance of sociality. It may be the case that such figures are media heroes in name and image only, but the contemporary logic of popular politics seems to dictate that that's good enough.

For other political aspirants, the Westerner image can be the kiss of death, since in some circles such identification smacks of sexism and warmongering, not to mention simplemindedness. But the domestic dimension of political heroism cannot be ignored virtually everywhere. It is true that some male political figures have "sex appeal" but only vicariously and not openly. (One thinks of Robert Redford's wife in *The Candidate* remarking that he would succeed in politics because he's got "the power.") But there is still a strong expectation of domestic romance among public aspirants, that the male candidate, for instance, be a "family man." Gary Hart's domestic image, and his Presidential hopes, evaporated when his extramarital proclivities were revealed (including a cover photo in *The National Inquirer* with a curvaceous blonde, who was decidedly not his wife, on his lap). The political hero's adventures occur outside the home, and serve the community's welfare; thus his sexual adventures must restrict themselves to marital fidelity. The familiar pretense of familial bliss that we see in campaign propaganda speaks to this expectation, derived directly from the myth of domestic romance. Much effort is expended to assure us that the "First Family" is happy and close, even if (as we discovered eventually with the Reagans) that is not the case. But in politics, it is often true that people want to see myths confirmed, including that the mighty and great share the same mythology of domestic romance that we do. For this reason, political wives are often portrayed in women's magazines as a Cinderella story, now (as First Lady, for instance) living in a palace with Prince Charming.[7] Whatever political adventures engage the Prince outside of the palace, the patina of romance must pervade his domestic quarters.

The Hero of Mystery

In many ways the Western story is basically a founding myth, a popular folktale of the adventure of our forefathers in creating American civilization out of the wilderness. The myth of domestic romance is the civilized successor to the founding, through the creation of the Town and the domestic romance at its core that sustains the familial core of civilization. In a sense the myth of the happy domesticated father at home is a sustaining myth. Both have great political relevance in the public representation of the political hero. But Cawelti deals with another popular formula with mythic overtones, the myth of the hero of mystery. In popular iconography, the prototypical figure of Western adventure is the gunfighter; the icon of the domestic romance is the husband-townsman. But the paradigmatic figure of mystery is the private detective. For the detective, there is no frontier to which one might venture; there is no bourgeois complacency of the home and town; there is the mystery of the city, the urban nighttown and structures of power that he investigates. The Western hero's power stems from his use of violence against wild savagery to create civilization; the domestic romantic hero's power comes from his use of persuasion against social ills (pettiness, greed, ignorance) in order to sustain the peaceable community. The hero of mystery—a private eye, rogue cop, or some other kind of investigator—is neither adventurer nor romantic; he is not of the great outdoors nor of the town, but rather of the city. Unlike these other legacies of popular heroics, he has few political counterparts, and indeed is more likely apolitical or antipolitical.

The divorce of the private detective from politics is part of his alienation from society. He is an alien in the sense of independence and suspicion: society has not become civilized, and violence is everywhere; beneath the complacent veneer of domestic respectability lurks dark secrets and bestial acts. The American private eye inherits from his European predecessors (Sherlock Holmes, Lord Peter Wimsey, Hercule Poirot) the power of ratiocination, the ability to solve mysteries through investigative skill. But he adds to that the power of survival, an existential sense that the modern world is a hostile and unforgiving place, and that the individual survives through a kind of private political skill. In an important way, the American private eye (Sam Spade, Phillip Marlowe, Jake Giddes of *Chinatown* and *The Two Jakes*) is a Machiavellian figure attempting to make do in a Hobbesian world. The "civic individualism" of the private detective is that of the loner, the outsider, the streetwise realist devoid of romantic illusions or social commitments. He realizes that he is up against society's elaborate fabric of lies, and that the core of personality and society is the secret. His power of investigation leads him into trying to demystify secrets, while realizing that he only scratches the surface of the social mystery and the heart of darkness just beneath the surface. He is an ironic hero, aware of the absurd in what he sees and reveals, but also clear that what he uncovers in knowledge of evil.

The private detective, then, is a solitary and anti-heroic actor in a public world of decaying values and social order, symbolized by the labyrinth city in which he dwells. He is also antisocial, in that he believes social power is always in conflict with the free individual. He defines freedom as freedom from government, his ability to survive his forays into the mazeways of power while retaining his autonomy and integrity. His political ethos is pragmatic and expedient, operating while making no ethical judgements nor moral assumptions. He wants answers, but is sure he will get only a few answers, and certainly not The Answer. He is a mythic figure who wants to debunk all our myths, a figure of our popular dreams who wants to disabuse us of our dreams. Reality is too real, and knowledge altogether too unknowable for him to live with illusions, since such wishful thinking threatens his life and liberty. He believes in his own individual rationality but certainly not social rationality nor civil rationality in government. His attitude toward politicians and government (the police, for example) is one of contempt. He does not believe in "the political illusion," the idea that politics will solve our problems. The conquests of the political adventurer (warfare, for example, or "wars" on poverty or drugs) are so much bombast, and the solutions of the domestic political romantic (reformers, for instance) desperate efforts to convince themselves that society is operable and benevolent, when in fact "solutions" are part of the problem, and "plans" in fact nothing but blue smoke and mirrors. Organized power for him is at the heart of a heartless world, something that must be circumvented in order to survive. The mythic frontier and the equally mythic town have a sacral quality, blessing a formed and sustained community that is sacrosanct. The detective stalks an urban landscape that is thoroughly profane and hopelessly corrupt, a condition with which he must live since there is no exit

There are, of course, many variations on the detective genre.[8] In the movies alone, one can find not only the classical Hammett-Chandler characters, but also the existential variant of the private citizen thrown into the investigation of an evil that the authorities cannot or will not discover. Alfred Hitchcock brought great formulation to "the wrong man," someone wrongly accused who must on his own uncover the awful truth (*The Thirty-Nine Steps, The Lady Vanishes, The Man Who Knew Too Much, North by Northwest, Frenzy,* and so on). But he also included other mysteries investigated by private individuals without official help: the bedridden photographer of *Rear Window* who realizes that he has witnessed a murder, and the retired cop of *Vertigo* who becomes an integral part of a baffling puzzle himself. And there are many other variants: in *Citizen Kane,* the reporter seeks the mystery of "Rosebud"; in *D.O.A.,* a doomed man hunts for his own killers; in *Silkwood,* a nuclear worker attempts to discover the truth of nuclear pollution; in *The China Syndrome* reporters try to penetrate the mystery of nuclear plant safety; in *Blue Velvet,* teenagers discover the ghastly truth about the lower world beneath suburban calm and light. In classical *film noir* (the dark movies), people were often caught in tangled webs of deception and betrayal that only someone with investigative talents can untangle. The urbane and cynical Sam Spade or Phillip Marlowe (Humphrey Bogart of *The Big Sleep* and *The Maltese Falcon*) moved through a shadowy world of dark and mean streets and motives. Jake Giddes (Jack Nicholson) of *Chinatown* and *The Two Jakes* focused his critical eye on the hidden forces behind the control of the elemental need for water and discovers a secret even more elemental and dark. But in all cases, what truth is uncovered stems from the exercise of a critical eye, someone willing to look into things. We might say that the Western adventurer exercises an active eye; the domestic romantic hero exercises a sentimental eye; and the private eye observes and inquires into, or critiques, the Hobbesian "kingdom of darkness."

In politics, it has been our habit to select leaders who conform to some of the mythic imagery of the adventurer and the romantic. We have shied away from figures who project connection with such a critical stance about society. The closest we come is admiration for the investigative reporter who uncovers political corruption, as with the Woodward and Bernstein characters of *All the President's Men*. But even that is not universal nor permanent, and indeed it can be argued that during the 1980s there was a general antipathy toward serious and probing inquiry into corruption and malfeasance, even though the Reagan Administration acquired a reputation for widespread "sleaze" and major scandal. Attacks on the press suggested a public mood of wishing to believe in positive mythology again, exalting the images of the Western adventurer and the happy romantic at home. Admiration for the investigator came from those who think that politics is a sham and con, and that those in power have something to hide. The private eye of whatever stripe is in a public sense powerless, in that he seeks no power and indeed cedes it to the mighty; but in another sense he is a hero of private power, the power of the civil individual to survive in an uncivil society. The private eye sees through a glass, darkly; but at least he is willing to look, and is not afraid of what he might see.

These heroic images have hitherto been largely male-dominated roles. But now both in fiction and actuality women have entered former male bastions of heroic endeavor. For example, the Sigourney Weaver character in *Aliens* is in the tradition of heroic adventure into an unknown frontier, with the defeat of the alien force through violence (actually genocide!). We will no doubt see more "space Westerns" and similar formulas that include women in adventures, such as warfare, space exploration, and "post-civilization" fantasies in futuristic wastelands. Too, we will no doubt see women portrayed in romantic roles that treat their attempt to combine home and work, family and career. A film such as *Working Girl* depicts such an upward-mobile struggle to find both the right man and corporation, but told from the point of view of the female heroine. Finally, we already see women private detectives and cop teams (V.I. Warshawski, *Cagney and Lacey*) at work in an urban environment, and undoubtedly as female independence, and perhaps disillusionment with the power structure, grows, women will find uses for the critical stance implied by the detective hero, and the political existentialism such a stance recommends.

Conclusion

Here we have discussed some of the ways that American monomyths—the myth of the Western adventurer, the myth of the domestic romantic, and the myth of the private detective—have heroic relevance to politics. Such heroic myths are not idle fantasies, but have real-world consequences. The Achilles heel of the Western adventurer is the belief in violent solutions that can lead to Vietnams and nuclear war; similarly, the domestic hero may believe too easily in the stultifying conformity and debasing pursuit of consumption that characterizes much of bourgeois life. The private detective courts the danger of cynicism, believing that everything is corrupt beyond redemption, and that the individual is radically alienated and alone. Yet all three heroic stances have survived because they have their merits. But we may wonder if they are sufficient mythic ground for heroic figures in the twenty-first century. Heroism, after all, is only heroic if it in some way succeeds in offering political actors a role structure as to what to act for in political dramas. If our ancient mythic heritage proves inadequate for the brave new world of the future that is quickly upon us, then it may be the case that we will find new myths and new heroes (perhaps old ones in new guise) on which we can base action for a new political time.

Chapter Four
Popular Sports and Politics

As the previous chapter indicated, heroic fictions and figures have different popular origins and conceptions. Although the Westerner, the townsman, and the private detective stem from different historical roots, their mythologization made them into enduring heroic types that still find uses for. Indeed, those three heroes correspond with the three major popular ways of life in our history: life on the frontier where heroic defense against natural threats was important; the growth of settled "island communities" where the maintenance of good social relations was paramount; and the growth and even decay of the city, where understanding the rules of existential survival was crucial. All of these kinds of fictional heroes were important for both mythic and romantic understanding. Their correspondence with factual heroes was always quite tenuous, but their function was clear in offering us guideposts for heroic action. In politics, what we expect the Westerner and the romantic townsman to do remains important for political heroism.

There is, however, another important source of heroism with popular roots: sports. The rudimentary games Americans began to play in colonial days would be passed on from generation to generation as part of folk tradition. The old game of "rounders," for instance, evolved into baseball. Baseball swept across the nation after the Civil War, and in the latter part of the nineteenth century practically every urban neighborhood and every rural town had a baseball team. Professional leagues began to appear, and the rest, as they say, is history: baseball eventually became "the summer game," the massively rich sport played in huge sports stadiums and followed by many millions as a central part of our popular life. Those outstanding players of long ago who were local heroes are now superseded by players who are heroes to great multitudes of fans, and are paid enormous sums for the efforts. In baseball

63

as well as in other major sports, we have come to venerate the sport as socially valuable, and to celebrate the player as a social hero. Early on in the history of sports, a popular literature began to appear promoting athletes, both real and fictional, to heroic status. The dime novels recounting the exploits of Frank Merriwell and like heroes, as well as the rise of sportswriting, did much for the mythologization of both the sport and the ideal of the hero-athlete. Since then, much has been written about the meaning of sports for Americans. Baseball in particular has been conceived as a mythic metaphor for the American Dream, a sanctified place that has a kind of redemptive purity. This was never expressed better than in the 1989 film *Field of Dreams* (based on the W.P. Kinsella novel *Shoeless Joe*), in which baseball is used as a pastoral metaphor for social and political reconciliation between generations, races, and ideologies. Such mythic celebration reminds us that we can expand the oft expressed notion of the cultural, and here political, importance of baseball to include all sports. If you want to understand America, study sports.

The Dream of Fields

If our thesis is correct that those popular dramas that emerge from folk tradition into mass culture are important sources of learning, then sport is clearly worth understanding. For sports allow a political culture the considerable luxury of pure enactment of mythic values, in a dream-context wherein the "field" is unsullied by the compromises and confusions of reality. It is for this reason that sports are not only venerated and protected, but also given a ritual quality. The World Series, Super Bowl, or NCAA Final Four occur under the symbolic canopy of quasi-religious legitimization. Such mega-events are heavily hyped for crass economic reasons, to be sure, but they are also exalted as significant cultural rituals enveloped in the language and procedure of ritual affirmation. The field of play is not just a game, but a sacralized place where highly symbolic actions serve as a metaphor for social values and practices.

A socially significant metaphor "carries" meaning from one familiar and concrete context to another that is more inclusive or difficult to grasp. Sports serve a society as a ritual drama with inclusive metaphorical meaning. And the infusion of games with meaning is not confined just to the large-scale, nationally-shared events. Rather the "lessons of sports" are communicated very early in life. We discovered even before school that playing is fun, and were anxious to prove ourselves. In school, it was soon clear that the institution valued athletic achievement, and we acquired local heroes we admired and even emulated. Further, learning the value of sports led us to follow the exploits of the major leagues, and the sports heroes who dominate those leagues. We talked sports, tried to play them, aped the mannerisms of our heroes, even won letters, or became cheerleaders and pom-pom girls, and imagined glory days on the field of our own private dreams. Sports became for many of us a metaphorical world where we could first "try out" our abilities, engage in physical competition and cooperation, and come to grips with our own heroism, or in most cases, the lack of it.

We also learned very quickly that most of us are not very good at sports. Yet the fact that we are largely relegated to the role of spectator does not seem to lessen the value we as a society place on sports. Sport is a metaphor we live by, offering us a universe of discourse all its own, but holding meaning for the rest of our lives. We can thus value it both as an area of pure play for its own sake, and also as play with valuable life lessons applicable for "the game of life." It is no accident, then, that the rhetoric of sports is an integral part of our popular language. We speak of political campaigns as a "horse race," with the candidates "jockeying for position," ready to be "first out of the gate," and with the stamina for "the stretch run." We admire businesspersons who are able to "play hardball" or are willing to "carry the ball." We even speak in male groups of a sexual exploiter of women as someone who "scores a lot." Even if many of us only participate in the action vicariously, the life lesson is that passive participation is legitimate and proper for most of us. Sports as an elite activity involving the action of only a few talented players who dominate the field of play serves as a metaphor of this hierarchical separation in non-sporting fields of play. If we are expected to defer to the heroes of the playing field, then this is easily transferred to fields of endeavor other than athletics. From this social interpretation, sports teaches us that heroism is restricted to the talented few able to enter the arenas of bigtime business, academia, or politics, with most of us restricted to the role of spectator who can only audit the action.

This use of sports is counterbalanced by the metaphorical referent of achievement, telling us that like sports the world is a place where "dreams come true" if you "hustle" and "play to win" and accept "no substitute for victory." American folklore has sustained the myth of guaranteed success based on cultivating the proper positive attitudes and directing energy toward positive goals. No amount of empirical disconfirmation over generations has been able to dispel our faith in universal success. Sports represents for many of us a place wherein such dreams are vindicated, fed by the notion that if you try hard enough, you can make the majors. Even though only a minuscule percentage of the population can succeed in sports, nevertheless the personal drama of an athlete who rises from obscurity (and, often, poverty) to athletic achievement is deemed inspirational for the rest of us. Especially endearing is the athlete who overcomes the odds because of some lack (size) or infirmity (injury), "proving" that such obstacles are no hindrance to those truly dedicated to the achievement ethic, and indeed, should make you all the more determined to make your mark because of it.

It is often argued that this appeal to sports as vindication of the achievement ethic supports a kind of social Darwinist individualism. Yet sports can become a place in which a single individual can represent something more profound than simply his or her own success. Achievement can mean something of social or political significance. The most dramatic example is that of Jackie Robinson's entry into major league baseball in 1947. During World War II, there was much appeal to American black people to participate in the war with the promise that the values fought for would be realized for them after the war. After the war, there were the beginnings of rumblings of what was to become the great Civil Rights movement. Yet segregation laws still prevailed in the South and elsewhere. Despite the American ethic of achievement, equality of opportunity, and democratic fraternity, a good bit of the society was exclusionary, not only for blacks, but also for Jews and other minorities. This was indeed an "American Dilemma," and potentially an explosive political conflict. The first significant change in racial exclusion came in that most conservative of American institutions, baseball. There was considerable resistance to such an innovation, often on the grounds that blacks either really didn't want to be in, or couldn't compete in, an all-white sport.

Robinson's challenge was to prove himself on the basis of the achievement ethic. His stunning success broke the "color line" in baseball (and eventually all sports), and by extension the rationale for exclusion in other institutions, thereby giving impetus for American blacks to hope that their lot would change. (One may wonder in this regard how long it will be before the "gender line" is broken in sports. There are major sports with separate male and female sections, such as golf and tennis, and sports where the gender line has been broken, such as jockeying horses. But will the day come that women start at guard in basketball, shortstop in baseball, and cornerback in football?)

Achievement in sports, then, can have group, regional, institutional or even national significance. We are all familiar with the story of Notre Dame, an obscure Catholic college in Indiana which became famous and rich because of its football achievements. The many Catholics in the land who never went to college could not only admire the individual exploits of the sons of immigrant Irish, Poles, and Italians who excelled there, but also could identify with the place itself, as a vindication of the American Dream being available to even them. Too, there was a kind of class revenge involved: maybe we working-class Catholics can't get our kids into Harvard or West Point, but we can beat the stuffings out of Protestant Establishment schools! Regional conflicts include group identities, such as those of the American states, giving impetus to further "the pride of Texas" or wherever through winning sports teams, associating the state with achievement. Institutions such as universities try to make the same equation, that somehow success on the collegiate playing field makes for a quality educational institution. This has led to enormous outlays of money for athletics at the expense of academics, usually on the grounds that success at sports is an institutional achievement that "puts us on the map" and is quite lucrative for the school. National rivalries come out on the playing field in forums such as the World Cup soccer tournament and the Olympic Games. One's national honor may be vindicated by the defeat of a hated political foe on the playing field rather than a battlefield, an achievement truly the moral equivalent of war.

So in many ways and settings, sport is a field in which dreams are given life. As we have seen, these may be material dreams, in which an individual or a group enact a popular drama of self-improvement or group recognition. Since we believe virtue is rewarded, sports heroes have become handsomely rewarded, not strictly for their dreamfield heroics, but also for what they represent to people. In the history of baseball, for instance, there was a succession of ethnic groups that gained access to the diamond, paralleling their immigration to the United States—first, Germans and Irish, then Poles and Italians, finally blacks and Latins. For these new Americans working in rough industrial cities, sports stars drawn from their midst acted as dramatic exemplars of what they could only dream about. As always with those on the bottom of society, initially the only feasible way out of the slums was to achieve in crime, entertainment, or sports. Sports was the most morally acceptable as popular heroics that did not socially harm the gangsters or entertainers. By the success of one of their own, they could both admire and celebrate a paragon of the American Dream realized by a fellow ethnic, with name like Breshnahan and Wagner, Lazzeri and DiMaggio, Mays and Aaron, Aparicio and Marichal. The fact that such figures gained material worth in fame and fortune was for many proof of their worthiness. So sports heroes exemplified both the merit of economic individualism and the validation of group identity.

But the ludenic heroes of the playing field did not only exemplify the legitimacy and possibility of material acquisition through noble effort, they also became representations of moral worth. Early twentieth-century sports novels and biographies suggested that athletic prowess stemmed from moral virtue, a sports version of the Protestant ethic that propelled young Horatio Alger heroes into business success. The moral gyroscope of "inner-direction" was the source which guided heroic action on the playing field. Further, this essential morality made the athlete off-field a social leader who avoided vice instinctively and displayed the virtues that would make for his eventual success in the non-athletic world. Sports was a field of symbolic leadership wherein the virtues of play would someday be useful for the virtues of work. School children could be read biographies of Christy Mathewson or Lou Gehrig and draw moral lessons from their reputation for rectitude and courage. From the point of view of social authorities, then, sports heroes had their didactic uses as "role models" for youth.

Yet sport also had its political uses, as an arena of play in which the directed use of power is demonstrated as efficacious. As a political metaphor, sports has many uses: extolling the virtues of sportsmanship, teaching us about the universality of conflict, showing us the necessity of teamwork, vindicating the idea that life is competition for control of things, and telling us that the use of power is necessary to achieve the goals we desire. In this usage, life is a game of power, a game to be played by certain rules, but the race is often to the swift and the battle to the strong. The political virtues of the playing field (industry, cunning, strength, coordination, persistence, and so on) are the same that characterize the powerful in politics, business, and academia. Not only was the battle of Waterloo won on the playing fields of Eton, but also the many "battles" in worlds of power in which the values inculcated on the playing fields of youth serve one well. In many ways, the martial or "warfare" implications of sports is a masculine myth, teaching men how to use power in a patriarchal society. But now the combative aspects of sports are eulogized as useful to women, since such activity might serve the didactic function of teaching women about seeking power, or "the competitive edge," in a male-dominated society. From sport they learn they can play the power game too.

With such multiple metaphorical uses, it is no wonder that sport acquired a quasi-religious status in American society. The "field of dreams" becomes a pristine Eden in which the myths and values in which we most ardently want to believe are accorded dramatic legitimacy. Those heroes who engage in the battles of the titans truly interact in a dream-like world set apart from the mundane. The contest is "framed" by us in patriotic and religious blessings, giving it a ritual format as a prescribed universe of discourse that invites not only attendance but also worship. The "immortals" of the game are enshrined in halls of fame whereto the worshipful make pilgrimages. The huge sports colossi we have built even resemble cathedrals to which the faithful are drawn to participate in an important votive ritual.

Some recent films have paid tribute to baseball as the national sport that fulfills this desire for meaningful experience. *The Natural* depicted baseball as something that can be saved from itself through the intervention of a mysterious stranger with a magic bat who demonstrates the sport's power of renewal and salvation. In *Bull*

Durham, baseball fanatic Annie Savoy (Susan Sarandon) built a shrine in her house to "The Church of Baseball," urging belief in the mystery and miracle of baseball. And in *Field of Dreams,* an Iowa farmer hears a voice and sees a vision urging him to build a field to which the ghosts of baseball greats such as "Shoeless Joe" Jackson return to play ball and renew faith. Such depictions suggest that sport is a ritual of power, a ceremony of innocence that requires purification because of its sacred status and offers sanctification for those who believe. In that case, then sports may be a modern secular substitute for religion, offering the faithful a metaphysical world of magic and mystery in which the gods play and mortals watch in awe. We carry away from sport transcendent meaning, including the romantic faith that dreams can come true just as they do on the field.

The Field of Nightmares

If the mythologic of sports worship originated in the myth of Eden, it was likely inevitable that a nation committed to the sanctity of sports would live through the myth of its Fall. For many Americans over the last few decades, sports has lost its pristine innocence, and indeed has become a metaphor for what has gone wrong with us as a nation. The enormous amount of money associated with sports represents our descent into crass materialism as primary value. The various scandals associated with moral laxity in sports serves as a paradigm for our general loss of morality. Indeed, for many sports now dramatize the extent to which we reach for raw power through aggression, without concern for justice or mercy. We may have crossed an historical threshold after which fewer people believe in the sanctity of sports, having its mythic status and magical qualities. If so, it has become no longer a sacral activity conducted in a sacred grove in which the gods play, but rather a secular activity in a business setting wherein mortals vie for power.

The purity of sports has been a politically salient concern since the "Black Sox" scandal of 1919 (re-created in the movie *Eight Men Out*), in which several Chicago White Sox players more or less conspired to throw the World Series for money. The scandal was shocking to the country, and stringent measures were undertaken to restore public faith in the integrity of the game. Even though much effort in all sports was undertaken to convey the idea that the sport was unsullied by illegal money, occasionally something threatening emerged (such as college basketball players shaving points in the early 1950s). Yet, in more recent times, the popular perception began to emerge that the danger to sports was not so much illegal money (although there was plenty enough of that, especially in sports such as boxing and horse racing) as it was legal money. For with the growth of sports in the age of television, both owning franchises and with changes in the status of players (unionization, free agency, and so on), playing sports became enormously lucrative. A basic popular contradiction thus began to emerge: whereas owners and players saw their work as a business in which they tried to exact the most profit, fans still desired to believe that sports was mythic play, something untouched by filthy lucre. But this became more and more difficult to believe, as the economic motives of owners and players became increasingly blatant.

In the case of owners, perhaps the most disillusioning practice for fans was moving franchises at will for no other reason than pure profit. New Yorkers have long argued that Brooklyn lost its special place in American mythology when it lost the Dodgers to Los Angeles. With the many other shifts in sports since, many people have become aware that a team does not belong to the community. Those who own a sports team often feel no obligation to the city that supported the team when there is greater gain to be made elsewhere. The city of Baltimore was incensed when the owner of the Colts took his NFL franchise to Indianapolis. Popular logic would dictate that the loyal supporters of the Colts had a right to their identity of the Colts with their city; but the economic logic of ownership overcame any appeal to sentimental loyalty and urban tradition. (The great following that the Chicago Cubs enjoy may be because fans see them as irrevocably rooted in an urban community and loyal, if long-suffering, supporters.) Indeed, the demands that owners make to cities, threatening to leave for a better deal (tax breaks, a free new stadium) elsewhere, seem to many fans as nothing more than bribery.

The cynicism of sports fans is not confined to owners. With the extraordinary takeoff of players' salaries, and their often open display of greed, the extent to which athletes are admired for their "dedication to the game" is now severely limited. With free agency, players often left team and fans for a more lucrative deal elsewhere.

In all sports, the salary levels became breathtaking, and the sky seemed the limit as to what players would demand and get. Rather than paragons of team loyalty and deserved pay, now they appeared as freebooting entrepreneurs willing to play anywhere for money and making money at an exorbitant level. It was astonishing to witness great players who had agents making monetary demands for appearances even at charity functions, and such players charging money to sign autographs! It was in that new spirit children sought autographs and collected baseball cards not because they admired the player as much as an investment in a popular artifact to be sold just as the player had sold himself or herself. The new lesson of the material Dream was that selling oneself was paramount, and that money transcended every other value formerly associated with sports.

A related development that has contributed to the decay of the reputation of sports was the virtual eclipse of amateurism. Olympic sports has long been anything but amateurish, with nations contributing money and talent in an attempt to make a political point. But the fiction persisted that somehow domestic college sports was still amateur athletics. But with the enormous infusion of money into sports, and the fierce competition to win and thus gain money, the pretense of schools about the purely amateur nature of collegiate competition became more and more incredible. The lure of money was simply too great, since this supported the fantasy that sports "puts us on the map," provides great assistance for academics, and keeps the alumni and politicians happy. College athletes are competed for and hired, often sequestered in protected dorms, shielded from the law, and kept immune from the requirements of school itself. Coaches at major basketball schools usually have "school deals," making $100,000 to $200,000 a year to endorse a brand of basketball shoe, and require their team to wear them. The high price schools became willing to pay to win is exemplified by the story of athletics at Southern Methodist University, a respected and established school with a history of violation of NCAA rules, culminating in the scandals of the 1980s that led to their "death penalty." But there is no doubt that there are rewards for becoming an established winner: in 1990, Notre Dame cut a five-year television deal with NBC to exclusively broadcast their home football games for an estimated $20 million to $35 million.

The influx and pressure of big money in sports has led to calls for radical reforms. The president of the American Council on Education called for changes that would "break the insidious connection between money and winning...Big-time college athletics...is a professional game which poses as amateur; a big business which uses free labor." Further, "...rarely does any money raised for big-time athletics leave the athletic department to enhance the university community."[1] The argument is made that athletic departments have become the Pentagon of university budgets, a state within a state with a life, and inexhaustible demands of its own. In that case, both professional and amateur athletics may be suffering from giganticism, the dinosaur malady of being huge, cumbersome, and unable to adapt. Sport has succeeded in becoming a successful beneficiary of the material dimension of the American Dream, with colossal amounts of money poured into it, and becoming a major industry employing and benefiting large numbers of people. But in the process it may have lost its soul.

The New Sports Morality: Winning, Gambling, and Leisuring

We are all familiar with the sentiment, expressed most familiarly by sportswriter Grantland Rice, that when our lives are summed up by "The Great Scorer" it matters not whether we won or lost, but rather "how we played the game." Such sports rhetoric stemmed from the gentlemanly tradition of "sportsmanship," that a code of acceptable behavior should surround any form of gaming (horse racing, boxing, card games, fencing and dueling). The older sports literature had heroes who were "sportsmen," gentlemen committed to both competition and excellence, but who would only win within the bounds of the rules (and villains would lose even though they broke the rules). The morality of sportsmanship attempted to convey an aristocratic code on an increasingly democratic society, with mixed and limited results. But the idea that one should be a "good sport" on and off the playing field would persist. For example, in a venerable book about democracy, the authors wrote about "democracy as sportsmanship," including such attitudes as tolerating and honoring the opposition; being a magnanimous winner and gracious loser; and playing the game of life, and politics, within the bounds of civilized rules and norms of fair play.[2]

The ethic of playing well and fair is counterpoised with the ethic of winning. Americans are imbued with the "achievement ethic," the idea that we are "equal" only in "opportunity" at the "starting gate" on a "level playing field"; but in the "race of life," some win and some lose, and the people to be valued are life's winners, even though in fact there may be relatively few of them. The sports analogy also supports the notion that winning isn't everything, it's the only thing; that nice guys finish last; and that anything worth having is worth cheating for. Since life is competition, this popular logic goes, you have to fight hard, tough, and mean, forgetting any silly notions about sportsmanship. If the primary morality is winning, then winning at all costs becomes the only ethical rule. The alternative is that grimmest of all American fates: failure. Too, the tendency is to measure success by material possessions acquired, from money to opulent surroundings to beautiful companions. Success is measured by your "score" in wealth over visible objects, and exists as conspicuous proof of your individual worth. (Indeed, in recent years the business autobiography has changed from the older themes of the triumph of moral rectitude in an "inner-directed" captain of industry or the triumph of organizational skill by an "other-directed" corporate executive to the triumph of an individual entrepreneur who is simply more amoral—being a bigger S.O.B. than his or her competitors—ruthlessly using and abandoning employees and corporations.)

In the world of those on "Lifestyles of the Rich and Famous," then, utilitarian individualism is justified as necessarily involving you in barbarian competition, in an economic game without rules or quarter for the loser. (A book even appeared extolling the managerial virtue of Attila the Hun.) Too, the acquisition of wealth and power becomes occasion for flaunting it, showing off one's trophies (some successful entrepreneurs of recent times acquired young and beautiful "trophy wives," abandoning their older wives). Rather than acting as paragons of the responsible use of wealth, many of the rich used wealth for the ostentatious display of their loot, with expressions of contempt for those unwilling or unable to become rich and famous. Similarly, many contemporary sports heroes display the same boorish and self-important behavior, since their achievements make them equally above conventional rules of conduct. An extraordinary athlete is deemed another version of the elite of life's "winners." They are part of the celebrity culture for whom the ordinary rules do not seem to apply, wherein behavior we might find intolerable at home or at work we now expect.

On the other hand, we also often expect, and relish, athletes who are part of the culture of winning to become losers. When a "high and mighty" tycoon goes bust, we enjoy seeing the arrogant humbled. When a movie star is arrested for drugs, we relish their trouble, although in both cases we cynically expect them to go relatively unpunished. Athletes in this case are often held to a more traditional standard, one that emerged from sport's past troubles and present travail. Wealthy athletes are as given to indulgence as other of life's winners, yet standards of purity and innocence remain so strong among the sports-minded populace that they are held to a stricter rule than entertainers or the celebrity rich. When athletes are exposed as weak or criminal—drugs and gambling in particular—we make a desperate attempt to restore our faith in the purity of "the game" by making the miscreant athlete go through an elaborate ritual of degradation and purification. To remain in the ranks of athletic winners, the authorities of sports must sustain the illusion of prelapsarian innocence restored. Similarly, when an athlete even of the Hall of Fame stature as Pete Rose is deemed beyond redemption because of his addiction to gambling, he is driven from the game, and the company of winners, as so unclean as to be exiled from Eden forever. The same sporting logic still applied to owners: George Steinbrenner was finally excluded from ownership of the Yankees. Rituals of exclusion demonstrate our occasional commitment to sports as a form of civil religion, excommunicating those whose heretical flaunting of the faith becomes too much to forgive.

Yet the traditional moral culture of sports conflicts with our increasing tolerance and expectation of expressive individualism. Central to the variety of expressive behavior is the leisurely use of money, including gambling. This has led to the expanding legitimacy of betting as a form of leisure, an activity given even more credence by the advent of state lotteries as a source of revenue. Whereas in 1919, betting on baseball, or any other sport, was the province of criminals, some of whom bribed the White Sox players, by our time betting was so accepted that daily papers ran the odds on games. State governments began to see lotteries, paramutuel betting on horses and dogs, casinos, and even betting on sporting events as an alternative to taxation, and initiated massive advertising campaigns to try to get us all to become habitual betters. Gambling has always been a popular activity (some estimates say that from $20 billion to $100 billion are wagered illegally every year), but now government sponsorship, taking it away from bookmakers and the Mafia, threatens to make it a test of citizenship: since the revenue goes for schools and roads and so forth, a good citizen bets.

Yet the consequences of government-sanctioned gambling we have yet to calculate. It may help create compulsive problem gamblers, undermine efforts at fair taxation, and feed fantasies of instant and easy wealth. Some fear gambling might undermine the work ethic, since it offers the popular promise (dangled before us in state lottery propaganda) of making it big by getting lucky. But this might preface the popular logic that such good fortune is the *only* way of making it big, so discretionary income will be directed toward playing the numbers or ponies or point spreads rather than savings or investment. In other words, popular ambition would be less directed toward working for a fortune than spending leisure time playing for a fortune. In a popular culture permeated with legitimized gambling, it seemed to many hypocritical to moralize about the compulsive betting of a Pete Rose, since government had now encouraged us to become habitual bettors.

But the legitimation of gambling may have a more subtle meaning and effect in the long run. The ethos of gambling might make many of us, investors and politicians included, to take bigger risks for bigger stakes. The public example paraded before us of those folks who have won a publisher's sweepstakes or state lottery for millions of dollars may just encourage all of us to gamble our savings, careers, marriages, and lives for ever larger stakes. This kind of risk-it-all attitude invaded the stock and bond markets during the 1980s, with disastrous results for some and maybe in the future for all. Perhaps we will become a nation of Pete Roses, wherein sports is interesting to us only because we can gamble on it, and gambling itself is no longer a sport but a compulsion. We can only surmise what the size of the national debt or the loss of personal savings might be then. Yet the rage to win translated into gambling might just do that.

A final dimension of the new sports morality is the expansion of leisure. We are a nation that is less interested in work than we are in play. We have been termed a "leisure state," a country that finds its meaning in what we do after work rather than during

work. Indeed, we feel an obligation to engage in play, an ethic
that has been termed "fun morality."[3] So we spend many billions
of dollars annually on sports equipment, and fill our spare time
with either watching or playing sports. But if sports activity becomes
a moral obligation, then it may take precedence over our attention
to work. In that case, our lives are defined by the quality of our
play rather than the quality of our work. We may neglect
productivity at work (quality and amount of what is produced)
for productivity at play, in terms of golf score, games attended,
hands won, or winners picked. If so, then fun morality has taken
precedence over work morality, and we have indeed become a leisure
state committed to the pursuit of pleasure. Sports might have thereby
become a corrupting rather than a recreative activity, since it does
not rejuvenate us for work but rather becomes more important than
work. We have expanded the "leisure class," an elite—the "idle
rich"—who devoted themselves to play, to include virtually everyone
with disposable income, comprising a society devoted to play.

This is not to say there is not a social and political hierarchy
expressed in play. For instance, almost all sports stadiums reflect
the class structure of American society: the proletariat in the cheap
seats, the middle class in the reserved seats, the wealthy and powerful
in the skyboxes. Indeed, there is more and more demand for sports
which are segmented into private enclaves that excludes the public.
Those wealthy enough wish to escape into protected pleasuredomes
which allows them sustained leisure. For instance, golf is now a
$20 billion domestic industry, much of it centered in the creation
of private golf clubs, resorts, and communities. The National Golf
Foundation estimated in 1989 that nearly 4,000 new courses might
be necessary by the end of the century to accommodate the demand
for golf facilities, including computerized analysis of golf swings,
golf tours (including jetting Japanese golfers over here to tour
American links), and building courses in Europe and the Third
World to expand the golf world, since by 2000 there could be 30
to 40 million golfers.[4] In other words, in the United States golf
is a growth industry attracting many upscale people who will spend
large amounts of time at play in restricted golfing pleasuredomes
rather than, one presumes, hard at work keeping the company,
and the country, competitive. Many Americans with money seek
both exclusivity and leisure, a state of frivolity that frees them from
both responsibility and serious purpose. If such exclusive play

becomes characteristic of the American elite, then we might expect that many amongst the mass will learn from this, and the same attitude towards work that the ruling class practices.

The attitude of "leisuring," however, is a habit characteristic of a self-satisfied and unambitious group. It obviously runs into conflict with the "driven" attitude of winning at all costs, and also the willingness to take big gambles. Perhaps the will to win and the willingness to gamble are more identifiable with a young and "hungrier" group than the settled elites of the late twentieth century. Demographically, the country is growing older, so perhaps the aging are drawn to golf as as safe sport, and the existence hierarchy of wealth and power as a safe bet. In such an aging country, the moral from the golf clubhouse is not one of achievement or daring, but rather satisfaction and conservatism, taking one's pleasures is a settled world where worry and risk are eliminated. Golf does not seem the typical sporting activity of a driven culture, one on the ascent; rather it seems one typical of a culture, and economy, in neglectful decline. Indeed, it is estimated that of the 4000 new courses which may be built in the United States by the turn of the century, over half will be financed and owned by foreign interests, especially Japanese.

The Fields of Power

The politics of sports, as we have seen, ranges from dreams to nightmares, from hopes to fears, from attitudes to actions. But since sports is an integral part of political culture, we should be aware of the many ways, both covert and overt, that it is related to power. The powers that be, or would be, find all sorts of ways to use sports as a means of political communication. This includes such uses as: sports as a setting for political ritual; as a metaphor for political rhetoric; as a political resource; as a dramatic microcosm for political conflicts; and as an exemplar for the felt necessities of politics itself, especially the "game" of warfare.

We all remember the extent to which rituals of the state are associated with sports. High school football games, for instance, include all the pageantry and pomp that give popular majesty to the symbols of state—the flag, the military, the national anthem, prayers for peace, hostage release, God's blessing, and so on. During hostage crises, the yellow ribbon appears as an emblem of freedom, and leaders of the moral community pray for their release. Indeed, during periods of political stress in which there is a desire for patriotic reaffirmation (such as during the latter part of the Vietnam conflict), such popular sports accompaniment—half-time shows at bowl games, for instance—will tend to take on a blatantly chauvinistic tone. Patriotism is not only the last refuge of fools and scoundrels, but also school band leaders. More broadly, such patriotic gore is part of the *spectacle* of sports, the extent to which we have made the "big game" into a socially meaningful event by surrounding it with symbolic pageantry. Since sports is one of the few "communal" events that draws the attention of significant parts of a community (from small-town high school sports to the Super Bowl and World Series), the spectacle has symbolic uses as a metaphor for the legitimacy of the invisible political community which supports state and leadership. In that sense, the symbolics of such events are rituals of power which remind us of the proper hierarchy of power to which the game pays obeisance.

The use of sports for political rhetoric, as we have noted, ranges over a wide metaphorical terrain, including contradictory values such as winning versus sportsmanship. But for the direct purposes of political power, sport offers a convenient way to express *identification*. Rhetorical identification presents the politician as paying homage to a manifestation of civil religion, the popular faith in sports. President Reagan had once played football legend George Gipp in the movie *Knute Rockne—All American* (1940), and used the identification with sports heroism to political advantage. (The real George Gipp was in fact a great if lazy athlete who regularly broke training, supported himself in a hotel suite with earnings from bootlegging and pool hustling, played illegally for the Bears on Sunday under an assumed name, and was never called "the Gipper" in his lifetime; further, no one knows if the "win one for the Gipper" tale is true, since only coach Rockne heard it on Gipp's deathbed; and even if apocryphal, Rockne may have used it more than once.)[5] Certainly such a tale from sports folklore and Hollywood fit Reagan's penchant for apocryphal stories with a homely moral and mythic adequacy, the selfless athlete dying young but an inspiration to us all. It allowed him to identify his own reach for political heroism through identifying with a movie-made hero, and the attendance values of "character-building" he attributed to Rockne ("He believed truly" said Reagan at Notre Dame in 1981, "that the noblest work of man was building the character of men"). Such identifications are often more modest, such as blueblooded George Bush asserting as a candidate that like everyone else, he had gone out to see his kids play high school football on Friday nights (Reagan, be it noted, never saw his son Michael, a high school standout in California, play).

Sports identification came easily to those who actually could make claim to sports heroism, a background that has become an important political resource. Politicians seek out the endorsement and public company of athletes, themselves basking in the reflected glory that someone they hope will enhance them with heroic magic. Gerald Ford, himself likely the best athlete since John Kennedy to be President (although Kennedy's athletic exploits were more scandalous!), cultivated widespread athletic endorsement in 1976 but still lost (nothing new: both Herbert Hoover and Al Smith sought the endorsement of Babe Ruth in 1928; Smith got it, but lost). Now athletic achievement can lead to success in seeking political office. Both former NFL quarterback Jack Kemp and NBA star Bill Bradley had successful political careers, often making the connection between what they learned from sports and its application to politics. Former major league first baseman Steve Garvey made overtures about running for office from California, but the revelation of his having fathered two babies by women while engaged to a third, and being savaged in a book by his former wife Cyndy, put a damper on his transfer from sports to political heroism. Other athletes have gotten the political bug, and the popular logic of it now seems irresistible to political elites seeking an attractive candidate: no sooner than seemingly ageless fireballer Nolan Ryan had become something of a folk hero in his native Texas than he was approached about running for public office.

The dramatic possibility in sports settings makes it a "natural" for the expression of political conflict, either in the rituals attendant to the contest or in the actual conflict itself. A ritual may become the occasion for public expression of political feelings, by boycott, demonstration, booing, or whatever. And a group or a country can "prove" something through victory in the arena over a foe with a political stance. American blacks made a statement through athletic feats in the 1930s against the racial theories of German Nazism, by runners such as Jesse Owens defeating "Aryan" runners at the Nazi Olympics in Munich and by heavyweight champion Joe Louis knocking out Max Schmeling. The American Olympic hockey team of 1980 thought they had made a political statement against the Soviet Union, who had just invaded Afghanistan and tensions with the United States ran high, by defeating their allegedly invincible team. The Cold War offers many examples of Olympic competition with political overtones; now that that conflict seems to be ending, perhaps the games will become less politicized. Such events as the Olympics could in a more peaceful world become a forum for the expression of political harmony, with peaceful competition amongst nations on the field of play signifying the ascendancy of economic rather than political competition off field. But that assumes a period of harmonious politics for depoliticized sports to emerge.

If inharmonious politics persists into the future, as many expect despite the end of the Cold War, we will see the continued use of sports as an exemplar of the political cult of toughness, especially with regard to the use of violence. For many politicians, the metaphor of politics as a "game," and war in particular as a "game," takes some of the onus off of mean or violent actions. A candidate for office who conducts a mean-spirited campaign with vicious attacks on his opponent can defend it by reducing it to a "game" in which you "give and take shots" as a legitimate part of the contest. Such usage defends meanness from criticism, since it is deemed an integral "part of the game." Sports such as football can be pointed to as a metaphor that life, and politics, is warfare, a violent struggle over things such as territory that enjoins hard-line, tough-minded strategic thinking and acting devoid of sentiment in order to use aggression to get what you want. Further, it allows elites who commit violent actions to think of what they have done as a game without undue contemplation that they have caused death and destruction. In this way, sports supports the cult of toughness, justifying to elites and the political community the necessity of using violence, but also making what was wrought to sound less deadly than it actually was. The philosopher William James once hoped that sports could become the "moral equivalent of war"; the rhetoric from the contemporary White House in defense of war-actions uses sports as the moral exemplar of war.

These usages of sports in politics in different ways intermingle the two as fields of power. Sports herein are an expression of power, the power to persuade, ascend, and force, a political lesson for us all. Even if that is so, this does not necessarily mean that sports is therefore delimited to male-dominated aggression. Women and minorities have found sports a way of expressing feminine or minority power. Sports can emphasize cooperation and teamwork rather than individualism and narcissism. People can even watch sports without exalting it into an event of monumental significance, since after all, it is only a game.

Child's Play

Since politics is often "adult" business, there is a tendency to give it popular credence by referring to it as a sport or game. But to reduce the serious and often murderous conduct of politics to play may be a false and misleading analogy. It makes play into work and work into play, confusing the realms of the serious and the playful. Making politics into play turns it effectively into something irresponsible. Further, it makes politics into a matter of gaming technique, "mastering the game" rather than attempting to maximize values. The game of politics becomes an end in itself rather than an activity that leads to political outcomes of benefit. In that sense, politics becomes child's play, something done without thought given to consequences. In that case, it becomes a political game without meaning, with politicians acting like children.

This was one of the aspects of modernity that the great student of play, Johan Huizinga, feared. He thought that much politically-inspired play was in fact "false play," such as staged pseudo-events. The huge Nazi rallies or American party conventions are false play, spectacles which are manipulated as "spontaneous" play but which are really phony and staged. Huizinga thought modern pseudo-play was sterile, since much of it was passive spectatorship in huge sports colossi reminiscent of the gladitorial bouts of the late-imperial Roman Colosseum. Such false play expressed a kind of "puerilism," evidence of an immature culture with people engaged in childish pursuits. Play is corrupted by becoming gigantic and monied, losing all of its fun. If it is the case, as some contend, that more and more people are "turned off" by both big-time sports and politics, this could be because they see both enterprises as remote and boring. For people who are mature, sports and politics may increasingly seem puerile, childish games that adults have outgrown. If so, this may help explain why more and more people ignore both big-time sporting events and elections.[6]

Yet the heroic fantasies that surround sports die hard. Many of us remember our "glory days" in sports, such as they were, with great fondness, and value the experience of the playing field (or the pool or chess table, or whatever). For those who didn't, now there are adult fantasy camps, where, for instance, middle-age dentists and accountants who are frustrated athletes can go to baseball "spring training" in a simulated camp along with retired major leaguers. Sports was always a part of the participant's "imaginary social world," but now they can indulge that fantasy by enjoying the pretense of both athletic skill and being a pal and equal of real major leaguers. Despite all of the "fallen" aspects of sports, many of us wish to believe in sports as somehow a magical kingdom that still is a source of sacral value. This is given dramatic illustration by the phenomenon of the "Field of Dreams" in Iowa. The film was a reaffirmation of the power of sports to offer us social rejuvenation through a pilgrimage to the sacred site. The actual site where the film was shot has become a popular pilgrimage. In the summer, many thousands of people come to the farm, and the baseball field laid out for the movie, just as the movie predicted! In the film, all our social conflicts and cardinal sins are forgiven: since the Black Sox are forgiven, fathers and sons divided by the Fifties, dissenters and affirmers divided by the Sixties, and cynics and believers divided by the Seventies are all reconciled in the 1980s, by the power of the church of baseball.[7]

Such a movie and pilgrimage is testimony to the potency of the myth of sports. Since sports may have dangerous childish qualities that tend us toward infantile politics, what we must do is build a mature myth that serves a mature culture. We need heroic ideals drawn from sports who serve as models of mythic realism. Unlike the movies or children's stories, these sports heroes are the ones who embody the ability to be heroic not only at sports. Perhaps the stress should not be on the exclusivity of sports as a source of value and character, but rather that sports, like other areas of life, reveals both limits and possibilities. To that end, perhaps sports banquets and pundits should tell both athletes and non-athletes about Moe Berg. Moe Berg was a premier scholastic athlete who went on to become a respected catcher in the American League for eleven years. But he was also a consummate scholar, graduating from Princeton *magna cum laude*, eventually mastering a dozen languages, and pursuing his interest in linguistics and language throughout his life. But he was also a citizen who served his country, leading barnstorming tours of Japan in the 1930s while acting as an agent for the American government, spying on the development of Japan's military machine. During World War II, he was an agent for the OSS in Europe, using his fluency in languages as a cover, and teaching himself enough nuclear physics to decide whether he should assassinate Werner Heisenberg, the head of the Nazi atomic program. Berg was the father of Japanese baseball, but after the war kept up his interest not only in baseball but also physics and languages, attending international conferences on both. Apparently he was "retired" but kept working for the CIA, and when he died in 1972, the importance of his wartime espionage finally began to be revealed.[8]

A figure like Moe Berg should remind us that one may engage in, and even excel at, sports without confusing it for reality, or believing too much that it is a guide to reality. Sports remind us that energy has to be brought to bear on any real problem, but also intelligence, language, and a sense of civic duty. Moe Berg understood the value of sports, but also that the deadly business of war and espionage was no game. He also knew that mastery of the world could not be done just on the basis of athletic strength, but required in addition mastery of thought and expression, and perhaps most of all, a commitment to the political community that the Romans called "civitas." Cultivating the memory of a figure like Moe Berg could remind students, athletes, and politicians that the athletic virtues are not enough; they must be complemented by knowledge of the world beyond the field of dreams.

Chapter Five
GODPOP: Popular Religion and Politics

It is one of the stock motifs of political rhetoric that Americans are a religious people. Polls can be pointed to which show that the vast majority of Americans believe in God, many believe in an afterlife and the divinity of Jesus, and majorities often agree with the idea that the United States is a blessed land, and support religious practices such as prayer in public schools. Many of us claim to have had a religious conversion experience, including several prominent Presidential candidates. We like to think of ourselves as "one nation under God," the heirs to the stalwart faith of the Pilgrims, remaining a "City on a Hill" as an exemplar for all to see the fruits of God's blessing.

Although eminent politicians and divines would like to sustain the myth of American piety, closer examination reveals that we are not as religious, at least in the traditional sense, as moral authorities would like to think. Many of the same polls cited above indicate that majorities of Americans do not go to, nor affiliate with, a church. Further, American religious belief, such as it is, is either jumbled or non-existent: many people do not know who delivered the Sermon on the Mount, have few doctrinal beliefs, and mix in elements from other religions, including the "old religion" of folk origin (belief in ghosts, magic, and god-in-nature) and "new age" ideas (out-of-body experiences, extra-terrestrial superbeings, parallel universes). Popular belief includes many religious ideas not found in the church of your choice, and reflects the fact that Americans like to believe in things, and apparently will believe in anything.[1]

The myth of American religiousness is further counterbalanced simply by observable social practice. The United States is a modern country that is the product of *secularization*, the historical process that makes sacral considerations more and more marginal or mythic, if paid political lip service to, and makes profane considerations

more and more central. Less and less do we as a people observe
the kinds of restraints that the sacred order used to be able to impose
on society: "blue laws," censorship, prohibition, restraints on sexual
practices (living together, homosexuality, abortion, and so on), and
the power to influence the attitudes and actions of their parishioners.
Many people in the course of this century have accepted the
increasingly secular order, tolerating behavior (divorce, for instance)
previously deemed unacceptable. Indeed, many sacral restraints were
abandoned because they were bad for business. This has led many
critics of American society to charge that we tend to hypocrisy when
it comes to religion, and that our true gods are purely material
ones. In this view, the true worship of Americans occurs in temples
of accumulation (banks), temples of production (corporate
headquarters), and temples of consumption (malls). Religion now
serves the function of justifying worship of the god of money, and
gets paid off for saying those things that support capitalist practice.

That may be too cynical, but it underscores the difficulty of
serious religious faith and practice in a popular society. For a
popular society gives credence to extreme pluralism to the point
of antinomianism, that there are no norms of thought and action
on which society can agree. Money may give people the freedom
to do as they want, but it does not give them the moral justification
to do as they want. In an extremely secular world, the material
community is exalted as the moral community disintegrates, as
"market values" displace moral values. The individual is left with
selling himself or herself in the marketplace, and expecting that
religion and politics will be marketed like everything else. To
survive, the sacred sphere has had to compromise with the secular
world of wealth and power, which has made some of those who
take religion seriously suspicious. Indeed, many Americans have
been attracted by those evangelical and fundamentalist churches
which have been the most uncompromising with modern secularity,
growing rapidly in numbers during the tumultuous changes since
the 1960s. On the other hand, so-called "new age" religions and
groups have grown rapidly too, offering a futuristic rather than
nostalgic faith that transcends the materialistic world of the present.

In any case, here we are interested in popular religion as a
political force. In doing so, we have to include all those things
that people worship, and those ideas they consider holy. Even though
we live in a highly secularized world, in which the role and even

the definition of religion has changed, there is still a widespread popular desire—"an existential hunger"—to believe in something transcendent. In a popular society, this will take pluralistic and often bizarre twists, but all religious experience and its consequences is our subject. Private beliefs about religion usually include a logic that affects beliefs and actions towards politics, so whatever is learned that constitutes popular "god-talk" can translate into popular "politics-talk." Let us look at this three ways: the relation of popular religion to the material order, the moral order, and the political order.

Living in a Material World

People who are religious have always lived in a degree of tension with the earthly world. Some have felt that those devoted to a faith should not compromise with the less-than-perfect world and should withdraw from it in contempt, since it is beyond redemption; others have felt that the holy should not compromise with the world by imposing the "rule of the saints" on the wicked. Still others, likely the majority, have made the sometimes convenient compromises with religion and the world, not worrying unduly about the contradictions between the ethical strictures of religion and the necessities of profane life. And of course, there is a significant minority, often silent, who think religion either irrelevant or a hindrance, and treat it with either contempt or condescension. In contemporary American society, the whole gamut of attitudes about religion, and its place in the world, obtain, making for conflicts between those who want to see religion become more of a force in American life, and those who resist that.

The difficulty at base is that religion, and more broadly religious and quasi-religious thinking, is in no way unanimous as to the proper *political* stance in the world. Since questions of the material and moral order ultimately are political, then the "religious logic" brought to politics will shape what an individual or group thinks should be done. In a popular society, popular conceptions of religion can become politically relevant if enough people believe them, and support a popular hero who introduces them into the political arena. But American believers are all over the map theologically and affiliationally, and thus so are their political attitudes and agendas. Americans have had plenty of sectarian-inspired strife in our history, ranging from abolitionism to feminism to prohibition to abortion, but since religion is so pluralistic and shifting, it has been difficult for religious groups to sustain faith in a political cause over time.

This pluralism can perhaps best be illustrated by the astonishing range of images of the "American Christ." Simply in terms of the material order of society, Christ has been depicted as an heroic capitalist, an urban reformer, a country boy from the sticks who took the sophisticates of the big city by storm, a socialist, communist, capitalist, warrior, pacifist, and ideal dinner guest. For Bruce Barton in the 1920s, he was the first great businessman, taking twelve salesmen from the bottom of society and sending them out all over the world to sell a product. In Barton's immensely popular book (still in print) *The Man Nobody Knows*, Jesus is portrayed as an energetic and gregarious American welcome on Main Street, and devoted to the entrepreneurial spirit, a career "worthy of the attentive study of any sales manager." In the 1930s, Christ was a left-wing "Comrade Jesus" sympathetic to union organization and proletarian fellowship. In the 1950s, He became a solid bourgeois citizen again through ministers such as Billy Graham who became His medium in newspaper advice columns. But in the 1960s, He became a radical hippie in robe and sandals, and in *Jesus Christ, Superstar* and *Godspell* leader of a counterculture group, and in a book entitled *Black Messiah* (1968) was "a revolutionary black leader, a Zealot, seeking to lead a Black Nation to freedom." Clearly such a mercurial figure is all political things to all people.[2]

In the decade of the "go-go" Eighties, religion divided along familiar liberal and conservative lines, but was much more fragmented over single issues, some of them moral, such as abortion, and some of them material, such as the just distribution of wealth and the enormous division between rich and poor. Perhaps most politically controversial was the allegiance of formerly "quietistic" elements of evangelical Christianity of various stripes with the Republican Right, a movement that gave fervent voice to a desire to "save America" through political means. This blending of religious piety and political partisanship badly split some mainstream churches such as the Lutherans and Southern Baptists, and brought a counter-force of groups such as People for the American Way. But by the time of the 1990s, it was clear that American Christians, Jews, and other religions were as divided on politics as they had ever been.

But it was their attitude toward money and those who have it that brought the visible new evangelical conservatives the most criticism. In an odd way, they revived the early modern idea that wealth is an outward and visible sign of an inward and spiritual grace, that those who have gained wealth are among God's elect. The "Protestant Ethic" of Max Weber's famous analysis was expanded as a defense of those wealthy who were part of the Reagan coalition on the theological argument that capitalism was "biblical," and those who possessed great wealth were entitled to it. This was combined with renewal of the old rhetorical tradition of self-help, linking Christianity with rugged individualism and the kind of "positive thinking" and business hustle, combined with jeremiads condemning "godless socialism and communism," "secular humanism," and other latter-day evils which have rent asunder the biblical unity of God and Government. The leaders of the organizations of the new Christian Right quickly found themselves courted in circles of power.

This newfound power and fame was heady stuff, much of it followed by money also. For those right-wing organizations, many of them highly visible on TV, found themselves showered with money from donors both rich and not-so-rich, for both political and religious hopes. Such wealth is not an unalloyed blessing for those with claims of piety, although their riches could be justified as further proof of being part of God's Elect, reward for publicly espousing the "biblical" Word about God and Government. Since God wanted "God's people" to live well, some of their numbers— Jerry Falwell, Jimmy Swaggert, the Oral Roberts family, and the Bakkers—lived in comparatively lavish circumstances (mansions, private jets, limousines, and so forth) and built empires (universities, amusement parks, crystal cathedrals, communications satellites, etc.).

Yet it was likely not so much their *elite* appeal—saying the kind of things the powerful like to hear—that built such money-gorged religious empires, but rather their *popular* appeal. If they offered themselves as an example who had made good, had riches and rich friends, rubbed elbows with the mighty, all the while maintaining their commitment to religion, this was inspiration to the many who followed their exploits on cable television. Their revived "gospel of wealth" not only justified the riches of the few, it held out the faith and hope in riches also for the many. If one believed in their religious *and* political doctrine, practiced the pieties of biblical faith and capitalist faith, then you could expect God's blessing. Some of the more prominent televangelists were accused of a form of holy bribery called "prosperity theology," with the implicit appeal for funds: look how well we have prospered here; we need money to continue our great work; if you send us money, you will be blessed; we can offer you examples of people who have been healed, forgiven debt, restored to their job, and so on from amongst our givers; thus you do not only support the general prosperity of the church invisible by your gift, you also support yourself in the material world. Although all the big TV evangelists denied it, all of them needed large amounts of money to sustain their large-scale operations, and indeed expand them; so in one way or another, the implication of material blessing was there. Too, the tendency was to cater to the popular hope—similar to winning the state lottery or a magazine sweepstakes—for some immediate windfall that removes one from anxiety about wealth and health. Thus the Bakkers most blatantly (with their background in Pentecostal folk theology) did not preach the Protestant ethic values of work and thrift, resulting in the prosperity of a small Elect of the rich; rather they expanded the Elect to include everyone who would put their prayers and money on a miracle, healing them physically, financially, and spiritually. The appeal was not a gospel of wealth salving the consciences of those with great fortunes and desired justification for it; rather the appeal was to those many marginal folks, some of them lower-middle class whites or retirees, who desired some kind of palpable help from the divine. "Given that the modern economy is incomprehensible to most people," wrote Frances Fitzgerald, "the Bakkers' version of the prosperity gospel could be seen as the cargo cult of junk-bond capitalism."[3]

Despite their quibbles over prosperity theology, none of the major new televangical operations created by Eighties television culture could resist flaunting their material success. Every Sunday broadcast, or mailout, or telethon brought new claims of growth, with new adherents, programs, buildings, overseas missions, educational opportunities, celebrity endorsements, and so on, all of which required more money. Falwell's Liberty University, Schuller's Crystal Cathedral, Bakker's Heritage, U.S.A.—all such projects that were evidence of both divine blessing and capitalist enterprise, since they were material proof of the earthly manifestation of the combination of piety and capital. Whether they liked it or even knew it, part of the appeal of the "electronic church" was that they were heroic exemplars of legitimate religious entrepreneurship. People were willing to fund them not only because they offered a ticket to heaven; rather more, it was because they were heavenly. They were mass-mediated shows that gave audiences a spectacular view of a "perfected" godly community as if it were heaven.

In the heyday of the televangelical showmanship, this took two distinct forms, exemplified on the one hand by the authoritarian and disciplined shows of Calvinists such as Falwell and D. James Kennedy, and on the other by the friendlier and easier "talk-shows" exemplified by the Bakker's PTL Club. The former showed a magnificent church, a dignified order of service, scrubbed youth choir, a prosperous and attentive congregation, all centered on a celebrated preacher who exemplified in his personage prosperity and gave rhetorical obeisance to the biblical wisdom of investment in both Wall Street's and God's stock. For Falwell and Kennedy's admirers, heaven is an orderly and quiet place that celebrates the fruits of God's blessing through participation in the primary group of heaven. But others, most notably Bakker and the Roberts clan, made heaven a more relaxed and even hedonistic place, wherein God's blessing can be enjoyed through conspicuous consumption. In its prime, Heritage U.S.A. was a kind of puerile heaven, devoid of Calvinist restraints or discipline expected of the faithful, and full of candy and shopping and a waterslide. Yet both the Calvinist and the Pentecostal heavenly worlds people watched on TV shared in common the feature of being a shrine of abstract materialism, a TV place that gives the viewer a glimpse of God's bounty to come, a kind of heaven's gate here on earth, sanctifying the acquisition of wealth and even the enjoyment of some pleasures here as part of the promise of God's people.

Those outside the ken of the religious empires that arose in the 1980s may wonder whether the Liberty Universities and Heritage U.S.A. places were shrines to a heavenly or an earthly power. Like the more secular forms of American capitalism that they justified as godly, they were committed to the features of the earthly forms of power—growth, affluence, technique, accumulation, new projects, success, and deference to worldly powers—all enshrined in the temples of their creation. Shrines dramatize symbols which make people come to the place to worship. Such new shrines celebrated their participation in a material drama, a drama of God's people to acquire the wherewithal to realize heaven. But it was still a heaven on earth, which always includes the possibility of backsliding into the worship of Mammon.

Living in a Moral (or Immoral) World

The rise of new centers of socio-religious power in recent decades represented only one form of religious attitude toward economic power. Throughout, liberal and radical activists who drew their inspiration from religion continued their criticism of concentrated wealth, and indeed of both the conservative evangelicals and "neoconservatives" (some of them former liberal activists such as Richard John Neuhaus) who they thought had become apologists for big money and power. Religious activists of all stripes will disagree on what should be the "moral agenda" of the nation, but they will all agree that there should be one, rather than a "naked public square."[4] What they are both pitted against, in some way or another, is the logic of popular morality.

The logic of popular morality is more prolix and less doctrinaire than the articulators of public morality might wish. It is also more accomodative and pragmatic, tending toward causistry (looking at the morality of something on a case-by-case basis) and Machiavellianism (finding and choosing what is convenient and expedient). Much of this stems from our popular tradition of "business morality," with all parties concerned with a situation calculating the percentage in it. For example, the moralists of a local community—ministers, teachers, newspapers editors—might develop a public moral logic as to why some innovation (liquor by the drink, say) is bad; but those who have an interest in it, think it good for business, or just like to drink will see it in different, and firmly popular, moral terms. (Similarly, moralists rail against the pernicious influence of X-rated tapes, and try to ban them; but there is popular support for such tapes, if rentals are any guide: in 1988, there were more rentals of X-rated tapes than voters who voted for George Bush!) In the same way, the American habit of individualism spills over into the moral realm when people resist moral strictures with the "who the hell are you to tell me what to do" kind of popular logic. This undoubtedly has always characterized moral strictures against abortion, and undoubtedly will in the future: like alcohol, drugs, or other forbidden activities, people find ways to have abortions even when it is illegal. That may be moral or immoral, depending on your point of view; but abortions arranged by the businessman for his daughter to be discreetly performed by his doctor friend he knows at the country club, or the country midwife for the poor, are done for very pragmatic and immediate reasons (the daughter's going off to college, or the poor miner's wife cannot afford another mouth to feed), if perhaps a "lesser evil" logic. The logic of popular morality may be condemned from pulpit and platform, but outside the realms of official morality self-interest makes a lot of sense to many people.

Even given the perspective of many religious folk that many such people, powerful or not, may be beyond redemption, and indeed even rule the sinful world, nevertheless throughout history there have been recurrent attempts to impose or awaken some kind of religiously-based morality through political action. Many political crusades in American history, either "liberal" or "conservative," have had religious roots, and derived their energy and direction from those who saw themselves doing God's work. Dr. Martin Luther King, Jr. framed his crusade against segregation in Christian morality; more recently, the activists in the "pro-life" movement and other Christian Right groups justify their activities in religious terms. Such "symbolic crusades" aim at "reforming" human behavior through various forms of pressure on the political system, from direct action (sit-ins, marches, etc.) to lobbying and running sympathetic candidates for office. But they also serve the purpose of dramatizing moral values in which the true believers ardently have faith. In some measure, it is being part of a grand *moral drama* that makes activists feel good about themselves and bad about those who oppose or ignore them. As part of a movement sanctioned by God, the believer can feel part of something larger than self, superior to the powerful few and indifferent many who accommodate so easily with evil. They admire and follow heroes who espouse and personify the good qualities that makes them superior to the world, and lead the moral drama to its reformation of society.[5]

The difficulty is that such moral dramas meet both political resistance and popular circumvention. The moral drama may win victories, but discover that society goes on unreformed—alcohol is prohibited but people keep on drinking, segregation is outlawed but racism persists, abortions are forbidden but people manage to have them anyway. In politics, one's values are turned into symbols used by politicians to win votes, but are rendered meaningless. Too, the more politically accomodative one's movement becomes, the more diluted becomes the fervor and spirit of the crusade, eventually "settling down" into normal politics. Finally, there may come the awful revelation that the movement has been used—by cynical politicians, story-hungry press, and hypocritical leaders. Stung by moral relativism and political compromise, many disillusioned believers either find another cause or retreat into quietism.

The two major political movements with religious bearings of recent times were the civil rights movement and the rise of the Christian Right. In both cases, the further they marched the more resistance they met and the more troops they lost. Dr. King was martyred and accorded political sanctification, but attempts to sully his reputation continued. The big televangelists fell more mightily and completely. With enormous television followings in the millions of viewers, and staggering donations (at the peak of their popularity, Jimmy Swaggert was alleged to bring in $140 million annually and Jim and Tammy Bakker around $129 million), they and the others were thought to constitute a powerful political force. The formation of Falwell's "Moral Majority" and other groups with political goals was viewed with great alarm among established "mainstream" church groups and political circles.

Whatever potential power the visible evangelical movement might have had was undercut by scandal and self-destruction. What was variously called the "Holy Wars" and "Gospelgate" included revelations of ministerial misconduct involving money and sex, intrigue and backstabbing among rival TV ministries, and eventually the fall from grace of Swaggert and The Bakkers (Jim Bakker eventually went to prison for financial crimes). Donations and viewership fell sharply, and the once ubiquitous "electronic church" had much less airtime than before. Politicians began to distance themselves from such famous clerics, and their political clout began to wane.[6] (There was always some doubt as to how much clout there ever was: both Falwell and Robertson are based in Virginia, but their concerted opposition to both a state lottery and a "pro-choice" governor was ignored by voters.)

In some measure, then, the moral drama of the new Christian TV stars was a failure. It was so not only because of external opposition, but also because of the spectacle that might have translated into political power, it could only be so because of their claim of moral rectitude that would let them lead the nation to redemption. Falwell and the others were heroes to some and villains to others, but the "Pearlygate" scandals transformed them into popular fools, objects of ridicule when their "holier-than-thou" reputation collapsed. For those who saw them leading a moral crusade that would transform America into a "godly nation," it must have seemed a nightmare. The "old Adam" in each of them got the best of them, a setback on the dream of the country becoming a new Jerusalem.

Living in a Political World

Religious beliefs, especially those propagated during the dynamic phase of a religious movement or revival, do have their political salience, despite what happens to particular leaders. We regularly elect to office politicians who wear their pietism on their sleeve, and indeed tolerate them having disparate and even bizarre religious views. President Reagan's remarkable musings about the imminence of Armaggedon occurring in our time seemed to upset few, even though he had the power to create a nuclear version of it. Vice-President Quayle and his wife were followers of a minister who taught that the world is under the Devil's domination, that Jews prove the "evil of religion," the United Nations and the National Council of Churches are tied to an ancient conspiracy going back to the Roman-Jewish alliance to kill Christ, and that one escapes the Devil by living near a protective "grace pipeline" defined by the minister.[7] But then many politicians, like ordinary folks, have odd religious ideas, and never act upon them, so it is difficult to know how seriously to take them.

We should take seriously, however, those religious ideas which constitute something of a political agenda. For many committed believers see themselves in a divinely-ordained *political drama*, a political theology coming to life in our time. This amounts to something more than the idea we are in a material drama as godly representatives of sanctified materialism, or the idea that we are in a moral drama reforming behavior; rather this is the more sweeping idea that we are in a drama in which the godly should rule, and make the State an instrument of divine power. Most recently, this has taken the form of an agenda which could only be realized in a "Christian America" governed as a virtual theocracy. Such an ambitious goal brings the believer in conflict with many values and practices of contemporary America, with the sense of fighting a "holy war" against secular society. An archenemy, the "secular humanists," have been identified as the agents of Satan who have conspired to ruin an American that they believe to have originally been founded on Christian principles. Because of them, the nation has fallen from God's grace, and can recover its lost favor only through repentance and renewed adherence to the letter of "God's law." Although it might seem unlikely that the United States Congress is about to enact the Mosiac law of the Old Testament (*Deuteronomy* 25: 11-12, for instance), nevertheless the Christian Right sees that as our salvation and destiny.

Their scenario of the political future (popularized by Hal Lindsay's *The Late Great Planet Earth* and other books) posits an imminent apocalyptic end to history and the advent of some kind of Millennium. Although many believers see this as the final mighty act of God, nevertheless they feel impelled to political action during these "last days" to participate in the apocalypse. This perspective informed the Presidential candidacy of one of the celebrity televangelists, Pat Robertson, who ran in 1988 and maintained his interest in running thereafter. Although he affirmed much of the Christian Right perspective in a call for the renewal of "traditional values" as the source of American power, nevertheless he vacillated on the extent to which he believed in a nuclear Armaggedon, and whether he as President pushing the button to start World War III made him an agent of God acting out the political drama of the end of time, in which, unfortunately, many millions of people have to die in order to fulfill God's divine plan.[8]

This less-than-optimistic scenario for our immediate future didn't help Robertson's candidacy. Too, since the apocalypse has been predicted since the days of the early Christians, skeptics wonder why the present should qualify any more than any previous time to be the "last days." There have been many candidates for the Antichrist throughout history. (Indeed, recently a retired Christian engineer attempted to demonstrate mathematically that Mikhail Gorbachev is the Antichrist![9]) But even among those drawn to ministers and churches which talk about apocalypse now, we may

wonder how much of such talk is just *religious play*. We do not
mean it is frivolous, only that rhetorical play with predictions which
interpret contemporary international politics as part of the signs
and wonders leading to the end of time serve important individual
and group functions. The believer feels he or she has an insight
into the apparently inchoate and random events and processes we
see in the news; and talking about it in groups enhances the shared
sense of knowing what is really going on, unlike the uninitiated
in the semiotics of prophecy. Too, as believers have always felt,
knowing what is really and secretly going on gives them access
to the divine and a sense of moral, and indeed, political superiority.
Since God's grand political drama is predestined, then it doesn't
translate as much into a political agenda as political theater in
which the knowledgeable apocalyptic believer can watch the play,
all the while knowing the ending.

If the Christian Right did somehow prevail politically in the
United States, it would no doubt be a very different country.
(Margaret Atwood fantasized about this in her novel *The
Handmaid's Tale*, in which a theocratic elite running the "Republic
of Gilead" regiment women into orders, one of which is fertile
young women whom the ministers impregnate to repopulate the
country.[10]) Many people outside the movement fear the politics of
redemption, in which a "Christian America" becomes devoted to
the god of power and not the god of love. The "civil religion"
of the State, paying obeisance to religion in a rhetorical sense, would
be replaced by an official religion enforcing an agenda. Certainly
popular culture as we now know it would disappear. Many of the
activities we are used to—adult films, X-rated tapes, rap and heavy
metal music, TV soap operas, sexually explicit books and
magazines—would vanish. Certainly our sense that we had a degree
of freedom in cultural choice would likely go. We would change
from being a pluralistic to a monistic culture, with individual choice
being replaced by state enforcement. Not only would choices such
as abortion or birth control no longer reside with the individual,
but also what to watch, read, listen to, and so forth. Such a state
would clearly involve a repressive and even persecutive agenda,
potentially pitting the ruling Elect against the recalcitrant Damned
who just want to have fun. Such an America ruled by the Christian
Right saints might not be so "fascistic" as simply dreary and puerile,
excluding not only unapproved play but also creativity and diversity.

It is unlikely that a "Christian America" will come about in the foreseeable future, not only because a good many of us wouldn't like it but also because it would be bad for business. Even though the celebrity preachers and their organizations have been very supportive of big business, it is after all monied interests that have created much of the modern secular world, including popular culture. If it is the case in the future that both a populace devoted to its popular habits and monied interests with a stake in catering to those habits have any power in American politics, then a Christian American envisioned by some of its proponents is unlikely.

The Idols of the King

If American politics has been an arena of civic individualism, the kind of action we expect there has typically "framed" religion as politically relevant in only limited ways. A moral issue may enter politics, only to be subjected to compromise and cynical use for votes; a sincere desire for national piety and divine blessing becomes a routine part of political ritualism, devoid of meaning; and those motivated to enter politics because of a religious calling find frustration, failure, and even the lure of worldly politics, and its attendant sins—money, sex, deals, the soft life. Popular religious movements recurrently find politics the least reformable of human activities, simply because it is so human. It was not Moses but Machiavelli who defined the nature of modern politics.

For that Machiavellian reason, we should make a distinction between religion and religiosity. Much of what we think of as "civil religion" is public ritual and civic liturgy, the use of religion to shore up the state and politicians. Political rhetoric invoking God and godliness for state purposes is largely religiosity, the public display of political piety to establish identification between the politician and the religious feelings of the many. Such actions are not necessarily cynical, but neither are they purely religious, since they serve a very real political purpose that is anything but holy. When religion is so politicized, it is no longer religion but political religiosity. Religion does not set the agenda for politics, but rather politics uses religion as a political resource. Conversely, if a religious movement desires a "religionized politics," it risks making the State into an object of worship, a sacred idol deemed worthy of our worship because of its sanctified status. Worship of the State translates quickly into the worship of the political godhead, the leader who is the agent of the holy. It is easy to imagine a sanctified leader evoking a new form of divine right, certainly placing such an august personage above criticism and control. The rule of such an idolatrous American "king" would be angelic for some and demonic for others, in a state of truly religionized politics.

If such a state is unlikely in the American future, it will in part be because of the varieties of popular religious experience. As we approach the twenty-first century, American popular religion grows not less but more diverse and even bizarre. Americans now surely illustrate the old saw that modern man's problem is not that he believes nothing, but that he will believe anything. We celebrate many things, and worship many idols, mixing up rather easily what is sacred and what is profane. Lewis Lapham has written of our use of money as a "sacrament," "votive offering," and as the "currency of the soul."[11] Others have spoken of sports as our "religion of choice." If we worship a politician or a political ideology, then we have tried to make the most profane of activities sacred. The effort led by George Bush to make the American flag sacred by amending the Constitution to protect the flag from "desecration" struck many as a way to sacralize the emblem of the State and thus render acts of protest and criticism as political blasphemy. But for the moment, many Americans were too irreverent to worship the State or make the President into an idol.

Still, the many forms of popular experience that bordered on the idolatrous seemed to many observers to reveal a deep desire for the "re-enchantment of the world," giving transcendent meaning to something worthy of our worship and adoration. People impute sacral meaning in a wide variety of shrines, and make pilgrimages to perform rituals of popular veneration to new gods. Figures such as James Dean and Elvis Presley have been promoted to immortality, inspiring pilgrimages to Dean's grave (and the holy relics of his life collected in the local library) in Fairmount, Indiana, and Elvis' tomb and domain at Graceland in Memphis. The recurrent "Elvis sightings," including his appearance to people as a helpful angel counseling them in a time of trial, suggests a renewed search for divine intervention.[12] A glance at supermarket tabloids reveals the extent to which millions of readers play with the existence of the supernatural: demons such as Hitler are alive, stalking the Earth to further satanic powers; UFOs are in contact with earthly authorities and have established underground bases everywhere;

little girls get phone calls on a disconnected phone in the attic from their grandparents who are in Heaven; the power of crystals, pyramids, amulets, magic dolls, portions, herbs pendants, and so on to affect the future is assured. Nor is this belief in magical powers restricted to tabloid readers, or those desperately sick or unhappy. We have it on the highest authority that President Reagan and his wife, like many millions of their fellow Americans, were avid devotees of astrology, and seriously consulted their horoscope to set the Presidential schedule in the light of propitious and unpropitious times as predicted by the pseudo-science of the stars; and that the First Lady regularly kept on the White House payroll an astrological consultant, who was asked to provide metapolitical intelligence such as an astrological chart on Soviet President Gorbachev, on the occasion of his first meeting with Reagan. This might strike hardline Machiavellian realists as a strange method of political decision-making, but it does illustrate that the trail of popular religious experience leads right into the Oval Office.

The apparent popular hunger for a re-sacralized world is undoubtedly an indication of the extent to which the modern world has been secularized. Those who seek religious meaning and guidance in "traditional" or "fundamental" churches and movements and those who seek the same in "new age" or cultic groupings are all popular expressions of this need. As long as religious expression is multi-directional, its political potential is severely limited. But if the mass desire for religious affirmation were to become unidirectional, we could at some point in the future cross a threshold. This would be a moment when the power of God and the power of Man is unified in the personage of a political idol who personifies and heads the quest for political purification. Such a popular politics would involve much more than simply invoking God's material blessing on a pious nation, or attempting to intervene in political agenda-setting on behalf of some moral issue. Rather this kind of politics would involve a new level of religious mystification for a surge of power which could easily become demonic. The political mobilization of a hunger for "miracle, mystery, and authority" could bring to power new Grand Inquisitors who will use religion as the sacramental cloak of unlimited and vengeful power, rather than respecting religion as a sacramental restraint on power. At the moment, in the American religious house there are many mansions, but if out of this many

comes one mansion of popular political religion then there may
well be very real demons who stalk the land.

Part II
Popular Media and the Drama of American Politics

In the first part of this book, we examined some areas of popular activity with clear roots in "pre-media" culture. Popular folk heritage, heroic narrative, popular sports, and popular religion all had their origins in national experience before the advent and proliferation of the contemporary mass media. But they were not "innocent" because of their history, nor long immune from being incorporated into mass media which transformed them forever. Popular knowledge became something treated by tabloids, popular heroes the subject of dime novels, sports a spectacle unfolded in vast stadiums, and religion propagated in every medium from tent meetings to cable television. Indeed, much of the history of popular experience in the twentieth century is intertwined with its inclusion in the mass-mediated world which expanded and thus popularized further their influence. The triumph of popular culture as the modal culture in the modern world is a history of its incorporation into the media culture.

Today we may speak meaningfully of the production of culture. But we need not also speak disparagingly of the marriage of popular and media culture as something necessarily unholy. For the alliance of commerce with media technology was to give popular culture ascendant power, and indeed provided "the enabling conditions of a complex narrative art."[1] The various popular media we came to enjoy—books, newspapers and magazines, the movies, radio, television—in one way or another all served a "bardic function," since they have the ability to communicate to vast audiences a common, yet pluralistic, culture by using and adapting "an established repertory of basic stories and other artistic patterns."[2] The conventions of popular drama with which we are all familiar originated in folkish mythology, but have by now become the repertory of popular communication

What is more problematic is whether all the familiar stories we consume communicate a unitary, and convincing, ideology imposed by a power elite bent on propagating a hidden political ideology that reinforces the extant structure of power. The corpus of popular culture is thereby thought to perpetuate an "hegemony" over thinkable thought through control of messages, including the covert political ones that maintain the structure of power. But it is not at all clear that such an hegemony exists, nor that audiences are so uniform or so dumb in response that the message takes easily. Such a view assumes that the preponderance of popular cultural voices, even those controlled by big business (as much as it is, at least in financing and marketing), speak with a singular supportive story. But one of the many appeals of popular culture is the fact that it is against power and authority, is outrageous, ironic, contemptuous, and downright vulgar. Conservative elites or groups who desire order and authority may rail against it, but others who want to make a statement or simply a buck are quite willing to sell "subversive" messages that people want. For one of the many things people expect of popular culture is a critical function, telling them not only what officialdom tells them is right, but also telling them what their own suspicions glean is wrong. If elites could somehow enforce a singular voice through popular culture, we would find, one expects, only stories extolling the heroism of the wealthy and powerful, and the essentiality of accumulative justice; only dramas depicting the morality preferred by those in charge; and only depictions of the political wisdom and benevolence of officialdom. This might well not be the way that hegemonic powers would want it if they seek ideological conformity. But even if popular culture serves a *bardic* function, this does not mean it can easily serve a *priestly* function, justifying the ways of the powerful to many.[3] The stories of bards have never been confined merely to tales that praise the mighty. In such a world, we would not have the infinite of popular experience.

Since politics is an ongoing activity that occurs in the dynamics of time, these varieties of popularly-mediated culture offer us evidence of political change. Politics is an integral, if often covert, part of a great conversation which the mass media now "mediate." To that end, we will in this second part look in turn at some ways in which politics is depicted and reported in the mass media; how propaganda has become part of popular politics; the interrelationship between show business and politics; and the extent to which popular culture has become an international political force.

Chapter Six
Popular Media: The Depiction and Reporting of Politics in Mass Communication

We are all told quite enough that we live in a "media society." The variety of mass media are now for us something "taken-for-granted," often as a background to what we are doing (listening to music while we work) or as foreground (having fun at the movies, watching TV, reading a novel). Reflect a bit as to the "presence" of the mass media in your daily life, and you gain some insight as to how the ubiquity of the media might have an effect on how you think, feel, and act. The difficulty is that it is hard to pin down just what the effect is of something with which we are familiar our entire lives. Is the impact of mass-mediated messages on us non-existent, temporary, or long-lasting and deep? How are we different because we live in a media-pervaded world? Have the mass media now superseded other influences—family, church, peer groups—as the primary mode of learning? How has all this affected our perceptions and actions towards politics? Even if there are no easy answers to this, knowledge of the mass-mediation of our world gives us some idea of the sources of our images and conduct. To enhance our understanding, let us look in turn at three related concepts: media play, media logic, and media culture.

Our Mediated World

Think again of our daily media experience. For most of us most of the time, it is *play*. Media play occurs in the interstices of our day, a major source of our ludenic experience. We read the paper, watch the news, catch a movie, listen to some music, and so on. We are usually not compelled to attend to it, so unlike school it is not work! We like to think of play as a free choice, although much of it in fact is suggested to us through advertising or peer guidance, and much of it is habitual. There are definite patterns to our play that do not stem entirely from our own volition. When play is derived from the media, it is structured by what they communicate. The mass media are in the business of play-manufacture. Their job is to discover what people want to play with and sell it to them. Since they are marketing for mass audiences, they seek common denominators which they think will appeal for the moment. The mass media seek stories that will fill up our playtime profitably.

Media play involves an elaborate and ongoing social transaction we may term *media logic*.[1] This is the logic of media play: the creators and consumers of play find each other through media designed to capture and satisfy temporarily the desire for play. The creators of mass media play are concerned with how to use a medium to appeal to that desire. The consumers of the mass media are looking for media that entertains. When they find each other, the "logics" of both parties to the transaction have converged on an object of play—a TV series, a romance novel, a movie, a song, and so forth. This process has been termed "convergent selectivity," referring to how both creators and consumers follow the socio-logic of selection in converging on what is to be created and consumed.[2] Even though the intent of both creators and consumers of media play may be murky, the logic of the process has brought them together in the object played with. Thus what "goes into" an object of popular play and what people "get out of it" may vary. But it does create a populace devoted to seeking play in the many media of popular expression.

By so doing, in concert they create a *media culture*. This is a culture, largely a popular culture, that is essentially defined by mass-mediation. The media structure play in such a culture, but they also have large and perhaps decisive influence over learning. In a media culture, the power of the means of mass communication is such that it heavily shapes ends. If we define ourselves and the world through media learning, then we are not only a media culture, but also a media economics, and a media politics. The media culture floods our lives and our consciousness. Television alone has become a ubiquitous presence in our lives, with consequences we are only beginning to calculate. Perhaps the most important consequence is that the media, television perhaps most of all, has created an entire world of vicarious experience for which we acquire extravagant expectations.[3] The mass media create a symbolic reality which has features different than, and apparently superior to, our own immediate and palpable reality. In such a culture, we are "media-dependent," in that the tendency is for more and more of us to acquire significant learning from that new and pervasive source. If that symbol "the media" connotes god-like power to some, it is because of this potential as a *media mentor.*

The mentoring possibilities of the mass media includes our participation in "artificial social relations," in which "most Americans probably spend more time in artificial interactions than they do in real ones."[4] Even though the actual circle of those we know may be limited, the number of celebrities we "know" is vast, including all those who occupy the virtual media reality to which we have access. If we accord media figures superior wisdom and insight, then we may discount other primary sources of learning— parents, school, church, as inferior. We may find more admirable and advisable the "perfected" parents of a classic situation-comedy, the wise sage of a PBS interview program, or the dynamic TV evangelist, all accorded superiority because they are, after all, on television. More abstractedly, we like to feel we are well-informed since we have access to "news" and other forms of media information. Even though information and entertainment are blended together in formats of "infotainment," we feel part of the larger world of social issues and events by watching news and pseudo-news shows. Most all of us participate in politics solely through vicarious watching of the images and "sound bites" of politicians, news that gives us snippets of what's happening, and advertisements that espouse a candidate or an issue. Thus if it is once the case that many of us got our political cues from primary sources, including the local political party, now it may be true that we respond to the pervasive "secondary" source of mass media as political media mentor.

The mass media, then, have become a powerful and, for many, an overweening source of popular images and ideas about politics. Despite the notions that the media are intentionally biased and even constitute a subversive conspiracy, they became such a source quite unwittingly. They are still basically bards, sensitive to their storytelling function and to the social cross-pressures to which they are subjected. In both fictional depiction and news reporting, their narrative habit is conventional rather than ideological. In that sense, their media plays are stories that draw upon cultural mythology, although they may well serve elite interests or ideological partisanship. But they are storytellers within the ken of American dreams, be they economic, cultural, or political. This also means that they are aware at times of the extent to which American dreams can become nightmares.

The Mass Media and the Politics of Social Roles

Since the 1960s, there has been an ongoing struggle over the "proper" relationship between the sexes. Both the feminist movement, and the conservative counter-movement against it, defined the political issues in articulate forensic ideologies. But the mass media frame the controversies of the moment in mythic terms, as part of the ambivalent and contradictory heritage of the American Dream. In other words, media stories that touch on sex roles, as most do, expressed a wide variety of lines and depictions but no ideological conformity. Whatever "side" is taken, if any, placing contemporary issues in a mythic context makes it more palatable for mass audiences. And if there is, as some charge, covert "propaganda" in some stories, it is not as obtrusive as ideological preachments.

The common run of cultural stories are made palatable by inclusion in familiar *formulas*, popular modes of storytelling with well-known if malleable features—the Western, the detective yarn, the romance, the war story, and so on. A formula evolves from a national mythic heritage, and if it survives, ways are found by media creators to adapt it to changing historical and social circumstances.[5] A vital formula has mythic salience if it persists, and it may also have ideological relevance at a particular time. The proper relationship between men and women may be the text, or perhaps the "subtext" (what is implicit or assumed in the story), of the formulaic tale. In some cases, this inclusion may be quite unintentional, something rather taken-for-granted; in others, it may be quite intentional. But in all cases popular culture adds up to being part of the great conversation about what kind of society we are heir to, and what we want it to be.

Mass media formulas invite the development of *role stereotypes* and *icons*. A role stereotype is a depiction, either fictional or newsworthy, that fulfills some conception of how men or women should be at the moment. Role icons are more enduring ideas about gender relations and modes of action, although they preface the emergence of an immediate stereotype. Too, we may be heir to contradictory myths: the frontier myth can include the image of women as strong and functional people, but also restrict their horizon of action to domestic rule. On the other hand, that rule denoted women as "the carrier of civilization" (the schoolmarm, the church and reformist ladies) who were restraints on male barbarism and violence. There was also the darker myth of female sensuality aroused outside the ken of domesticity, through captivity, whoredom (as with the myth of the whore with the golden heart), or independence. With the advent of the myth of the town, there began the icon of Mom, the bulwark of bourgeois respectability and good sense. But with the evolution of domesticity, the image of Mom changed. Witness the changes in General Mills' icon "Betty Crocker," the Mom who ruled the kitchen of pre-modern days, but whose iconography is altered over the years into a more contemporary housewife, and finally now into something of a professional dietician. From the "TV situation comedies" of the 1950s and 1960s, one can see domestic bliss and the division of labor in the Anderson or Cleaver household, and the rustic simplicity of Andy Griffith and friends. But more recently, women have been depicted as single, professional, competent, and more complex (from Mary Tyler Moore to *Murphy Brown*). On the other hand, there are still plenty of domestically powerful women and domestically hapless men. Finally, there are now highly dysfunctional families (*The Simpsons, Married With Children*, and *Roseanne*) where everyone is slovenly and incompetent!

All this play with changing sex roles developed at the same time as the popular depiction of both males and females as attractive objects of admiration. The movies, for instance, perpetuated the myth of respectable womanhood and socially dominant manhood from the start. But the film industry also found widespread interest in the display of male and female beauty. Icons were placed in a variety of mythic settings—adventure, mystery, romance—to show us how the attractive could also be heroic. (Even the comic heroes had their chance to prove themselves.) What was considered heroic varied—tough, savage, chivalrous, military, patriotic, kind and gentle—but the stars gave us multiple models of heroic virtue embodied by the attractive. A John Wayne was the violent and inner-directed hero of the West; a James Stewart was the local hero of the town who brought community progress; a Humphrey Bogart was the urbane hero of the City. Jean Harlow was a blond bombshell as tough and streetwise as an man; a Katherine Hepburn was an independent aristocrat determined to go her own way; an Olivia de Haviland was the gentle and loyal helpmate. But such role mediation got us used to the idea that heroism was the province of those iconic figures who fit popular expectations about what kind of heroes we want.

Sex roles are a primal example of how mass-mediated role depictions constitute an integral part of our lives. Before the media revolution, we learned our role expectations from the traditional sources—family, friends, church, school, military. But our exposure to an array of media role models, both positive and negative, give us an entirely new and different source of what we expect to be and do. We are thus a part of the media culture not only by our vicarious participation in it, but also by what we incorporate into our own lives. We are all products of the accumulation of popular experience through the mass media as they have pervaded and influenced our lives. To put it another way: it is likely that we would be different in our attitudes and actions without our vast and cumulative experience with the mass media. We have come to accord those who are made famous by their appearance through the media as important in the conduct of our own lives. We believe it quite logical and "natural" that media mentors, figures we know only through "para-social" play, should have such an impact on something as intimate as sex role behavior.

Since the behavioral impact of the popular media, if any, is subtle, diffuse, and long-term, it is difficult to specify how it affects us. But consider this: a *Redbook* magazine survey in 1990 found some interesting sex role behavior among American teenagers: 8 out of 10 eighth graders have used alcohol; by 12, half the girls are wearing lipstick, blush eyeshadow and mascara; by 6, kids ask for designer clothes; by age 18, 44% of the girls and 64% of the boys have been sexually active. Not only are teens and pre-teens increasingly sexually experienced, they are also sophisticated consumers and much interested in making money.[6] Or consider this: for many people "you are what you have and can buy." In one study, young adults who were heavy media users were found to be much impressed with "the universally high esteem in which consumers of brand name products were presented on television." So they tended to evaluate other people in terms of their consumptive practices, thinking that purchasers of prestigious and expensive products possessed more personal virtues (e.g., friendliness, popularity, trustworthiness, punctuality) than people who purchase "downscale" products (generic or cheap goods). The study concluded that such people think of others on the basis of criteria of evaluation learned from the mass media, both programming and advertising.[7]

Such evidence makes us infer that people learn about what goes into playing sex roles from the mass media. If children on television situation comedies, for instance, are portrayed as smart, attractive, and "hip" mini-adults who are sexually aware and wiser than dumb adults, then they offer an emulative role model. Kids are now exposed to the consumer culture directed at them by the sponsors of Saturday morning television, as well as adult themes and concerns on the news, soap operas, and cable programming. Apparel ads directed at pre-teens will often feature "cute" depictions of kids dating, and kidvid programs will involve exciting play-lives, such as rock groups (the "Gems") and military or fantasy adventure. The National Coalition on Television Violence claims that the average child will see 52,000 murders and attempted murders on television by age eighteen (with cable and VCR rentals added, the figure jumps to 72,000).[8] If it is the case, as many experts think, that the lines between childhood and adulthood are being blurred, then the mass media may have a major formative influence on the conduct of social roles. The media may not be "directly" responsible for changes in sexual activity or a willingness to commit violence, since both youthful sex and violence occurred before the advent of mass media. But it may be the case that the mass media indirectly influence youthful behavior by reinforcing extravagant expectations. If media play with sexual activity—on TV soaps, for instance—is depicted as elegant, pleasurable, and without guilt or consequence—then the lure of sensuality may overcome more traditional and "puritan" restraints. Too, a mass mediated emphasis on physical appearance and beauty enhanced by apparel and cosmetics gives emphasis to superficiality, self-absorption, and dislike of those who are physically homely. There may also come out of such a "culture of narcissism" large numbers of young people who are guided by the fashions and cues of the mass media, require constant entertainment because they are easily bored, and focus entirely on immediate and sensate desires. (Such people resemble the rootless and amoral youth of Brett Easton Ellis' novel, *Less Than Zero*.)

The social consequence of such a change would be to have a society increasingly self-defined by the popular media. A truly "media society" would be one in which social roles acquire primary definition from the media, clearly a radical departure from past practices of socialization. Cultural practices such as sex roles, and economic behavior such as work and play, would be increasingly shaped by cues learned from media experience. Media domination of experience might mean that people define meaningful experience as that which is gained through the mass media (seeing a movie, watching TV, listening to music, and so on) and therefore give credence to the idea that the essence of life is entertainment. Popular "fun morality" would demand entertainment as not only diversion but also primary learning experience. As fun morality expands, work morality would diminish, leaving fewer interested in production but many more interested in consumption. If we create a society in which the central economic role is consumer and the principal cultural role is funning, then we will have a very different society from the past.

At the moment, such dire consequences of a media-dominated culture have not come about, since most people still work and learn much of their role behavior from more traditional sources. Yet these new expectations have underscored the popular dynamics of media play as a mode of role learning. Our cumulative media experience, from Hollywood to magazines to television, has made the lure of the cosmopolitan irresistible to many locals in small towns and farms. The mass media made fashion fashionable, encouraging folks at the local country club or kids at the local high school to adopt the fashions of big cities and movie stars. The media gave us a national "symbolic geography," places of glamour, fashion, and pleasuredomes—Hollywood, Broadway, Park Avenue. But most of all they gave us idealized role models, an array of culturally validated heroes, villains, and fools. Some were fictional, such as private detectives, Westerners, and romantic heroines; others were "real-fictional" characters, such as journalists, movie stars, and "cafe society." But altogether they constituted an "other-world" of new gods, more rich and varied than the gods of Olympus.

This is not to say that the media revolution was entirely "liberating" or subversive, only that both news and entertainment communications came to serve a *mediating function*. Larry May has pointed out how the early movies very quickly acquired a mediating funciton for the new urban masses, both migrants and immigrants, in their effort to learn how to adjust to urban modernity, and eventually for some, prosperity. In other words, the movies were not only a dream—like fantasy, but also a way to validate personal dreams of economic achievement and cultural enjoyment. But this was to be done through legitimate role behavior in "moral" work that is eventually rewarded and cultural play channeled through the reformed institution of marriage. In such a way, the mass media help people to mediate change through dramatization of the contemporary situation and idealized solutions. In a world of change, the mass media help people learn how to play old roles in new ways, and new roles in old ways. The early movies assisted people making the transition from a foreign or domestic Victorian world to the new modern America by giving imaginative life to the dreams of the populace.[9]

Since then, it seems clear that the influence of easily available mass media on the conduct of our lives has been magnified. Many critics have felt that American life has been so radically transformed by media proliferation as to be disruptive of all traditional patterns of roles, making us passive spectators of the lowest common denominator and vulnerable pliants for media manipulators. The media, in this view, are in control, determining both our consciousness and our conduct. We know, for instance, that heavy users of television are more apt to be afraid of crime, overestimate the prevalence of crime in society, and perhaps become supporters of "law and order" candidates who favor repression, punishment, and even vigilantism.[10] In that way, a medium has affected popular consciousness, and by inference, the political role of citizen and voter.

Such a model of media influence is not only unflattering, it is also too one-dimensional. The mediating function of the media is multiplicit, segmented, and interpreted by those engaged in popular play. That makes it difficult to trace the kaleidoscope of its effect, but it does not lessen its importance, since those things which are the most subtle are often also the most significant. It does seem fair to say that our plural views of our social roles have been enhanced by media experience. The complementary roles of consumer and leisurely play have been given impetus through media learning, but in a wide variety of ways unequally distributed throughout the American populace. Now there is not so much a "media culture" as many media cultures. Or to put it another way, the purveyors of culture who produce popular fare are not as universal as they are specific: one record company may produce many different kinds of popular music; one studio many different types of films; and many book companies publish many different categories of books for different popular constituencies.

What this multiplicity of popular culture(s) suggests is a society less characterized by role conformity as by role diversity. And, as Bruce Gronbeck reminds us, our diverse experience emerges from "meanings...made by individuals negotiating with...discourses."[11] It is in those various popular discourses that we find multiple negotiations and meanings, giving rise to groupings that create popular constituencies. Such learning contributes to popular self-definition of political role, in terms of what kind of understanding and actions one takes, if any, toward the political culture. The discourses of the media cultures of the American "quilt" (and not melting pot) help us to know the differentiations in political role identification, and how this affects the potential for cohesion or disintegration in the American political order.

The Politics of Popular Discourse

Who and what are the agents of media mentoring that affect contemporary political role identification? Let us look at some instances of where segments of the American populace gain important if indefinable learning that frames, through either "original" learning or reinforcement, their political perspective. Let us begin with the social segments with whom such learning is most likely to take place: the politically alienated.

As the political tides of the late twentieth century soured race relations in the United States, and increased the gap between rich and poor, there emerged racial and class tensions. There was evidence that many of the dispirited and deprived at the bottom of society were political alienates. Indeed, many socially conscious African-American and Latino intellectuals and creative artists seemed embittered by the negative turn of events. In that political atmosphere, a kind of street music emerged called *rap*. A good bit of rap music was about common streetwise experience in large underclass urban areas, often sexually explicit and highly profane. But some of it was also profoundly political, sung by young blacks and Latins appealing to an acute sense of alienation. Much of the political rap developed themes of black pride, contempt for the white Establishment and mainstream politics, and a real sense of being totally left out of things economically and socially as they stand now. Their political icon was not Dr. Martin Luther King, Jr. but rather Malcolm X, a more revolutionary and divisive figure. Rap music professed to see no political role for the disaffected minority, offering instead a stance based on black or Latin pride and the creation of a separatist mentality and political culture out of the ashes of the failure of the American melting ideal to "integrate" them into American society and up the ladder of economic and social equality. Political rap music saw only exploitation and cynicism from the system, and responded with a symbolically alienated stance that was communicated via music to a youthful audience receptive to the message. The rap mentors not only have minority constituency, they also have mass-mediated forums (music television, radio, and recordings) and a non-minority white audience. Even though there is undoubtedly pressure to "domesticate" or tone down the political rap message, for the moment it retains both its urgency and vitality. If it is integrated into mainstream rock palatable to adult tastes, it then may lose both its constituency and its power to persuade.

A glance at any extensive magazine and bookstand will also provide segmented popular fare that may well indicate a constituency for both political role identification and even action. For instance, there appear to be other kinds of political alienates out there, if one may judge by the consumption of magazines and books on war, insurgency, armaments, and male adventure involving risk and violence. There is an apparently inexhaustible fascination among some people with Hitler and the Nazis, military heroes and villains, and mighty struggles of arms. Gun and hunting magazines celebrate the power of largely masculine possession of guns and killing games. Even though organizations such as the National Rifle Association represent the interest of gun owners, there may well be a larger grouping in American society with somewhat irrational attachments to violence. A magazine such as *Soldier of Fortune* appeals to the fantasy of romantic paramilitary adventure in irregular or guerrilla warfare around the world. Such interests suggest that beneath the surface of civilized society are a large number of people, mainly males, who entertain fantasies about power, violent action, and domination. At its most irrational extreme are people who go crazy and start killing people with assault rifles. But such a "fringe" fascination results in people affiliating with right-wing or neo-fascist groups that do such things as train at commando tactics and guerilla resistance in the woods on weekends, join neo-Nazi groups that preach racial superiority, or become "skinheads" involved in racial attacks or desecration of synagogues. Such a covert "grouping" certainly involves only a margin of gun owners or war hobbyists, but in the right political circumstances (such as the Louisiana of David Duke) a popular movement of alienated males eager to assert personal, and collectively, political power through violence might emerge. If such a potential neo-fascist grouping exists, it has yet only covert expression in discourse in admiration of the cult of violence.

The discontent of the alienated or frustrated can be expressed in a wide variety of ways in a media culture. Talk radio, for instance, has become a forum for unarticulated discontent with the trends and practices of politics, with celebrity talk show hosts becoming the voice of many listeners who in one way or another seem to share a common alienation. The host exploits this shared rage with discourse that attacks targets who are deeded responsible for their plight—politicians, minorities, bankers, the hidden forces that are actually in charge, and so on. Such a media constituency may seem fluid, yet it can be mobilized on occasion into action. In 1989, when Congress attempted to give itself a pay raise, prominent talk show hosts from around the country urged their listeners to protest their outrage, to the extent that Congress dropped plans to implement the raise.

These examples illustrate the possibility of new political constituencies being formed, however temporarily, around a media outlet. They do not exist as a political force in the sense of an organized party or interest group, but nevertheless, they involve a grouping of the like-minded who can be mobilized into action by the right leader who can articulate in a media format their sense of alienation. If American society creates enough such politically-minded people, then such a "culture of alienation" could become both an organized and explosive political force.

Most media formats are neither primarily political nor specified toward catering to a potential political constituency. Rather the purveyors of popular culture usually wish to create a media constituency interested in an object of play devoid of political purpose. But this is not to say that political attitudes, and indirectly political actions, are not affected by such widespread play. They may appeal to "taste communities," or attempt to target specific potential audiences. In television, they talk about "broadcasting" (appealing to general audiences) and "narrowcasting" (appealing to more specific audiences), but in fact they usually fall somewhere in the middle. Music television channels such as MTV attempt to appeal to all kinds of different taste communities related to rock— nostalgic, soft rock, heavy metal, rap, and so on. Networks such as CBS and Fox attempt a "mix" of programming and news, ranging from raunchy to straightlaced programs and tabloid to respectable news. Although media constituencies are notoriously fickle and mercurial, nevertheless politically relevant learning is going on in these broader media formats.

Let us take as an initial example a venerable magazine format, *The Reader's Digest.* For generations, *The Reader's Digest* has been one of the most widely circulated of all magazines, estimated to run about fifty million readers per issue. The format involves culling articles from other sources together in a mix of interest to large reading audiences. Thus the magazine had to appeal to popular interests and tastes across a wide spectrum that was largely middle-class. The *Digest's* editorial perspective has remained vaguely "conservative," retaining its popular appeal by expressing the hopes and fears of their perceived audience. A typical issue will include articles about the power of personal will among ordinary Americans to overcome adversity without government help. The joys of mainstream bourgeois life are celebrated, evoking the myth of small-town benevolence and moral rectitude. Government is recurrently depicted as hopelessly inept and wasteful, creating more problems than they solve through clumsy interference in popular life. Although social problems are recognized, they are amenable to private and voluntary solutions without the necessity of government meddling. The *Digest* tends to be wary of change and the outside world, especially alien ideologies and influences which threaten the American "way of life." Articles about such political themes were often anecdotal, pointing up instances of government ineptitude or malevolence, foreign untrustworthiness, rugged individualism, and social harmony and progress. It is likely that *The Reader's Digest* has served a mediating function for many of its readers, helping to give shape to their political vision and expectations. A wag once said that Ronald Reagan studied *The Reader's Digest* as carefully as Thomas Jefferson studied Montesquieu. This was meant disparagingly, but the *Digest* did put Reagan in touch with a media format that expressed political sensibilities common to many Americans who instinctively think of themselves as "conservative," patriotic, and pious, and dislike or fear those who flaunt the myths and values associated with their way of life. *The Reader's Digest* provided popular vindication of the canons of middle-class normalcy, and became both a mythic and ideological forum useful for the political purposes of American conservatism. Reagan's acquaintance with the way of life the *Digest* represented served him better in popular politics than studying Montesquieu.

There are many news formats which acquire media constituencies. Network news, "tabloid" news, interview and investigatory formats all have their followings. But exposure to news formulas may not only affect our "information" about politics, it may also affect our perceptions of politics, how we "frame" the political world. News, after all, is another form of popular programming, selected and dramatized in order to attract audiences. If it becomes a habit, a news format then acquires for the inhabiter the status of credibility. Popular acceptance of the credibility of a news program (e.g., the *CBS Evening News*) and news personage (Dan Rather) gives it "truth-value" ("It's not the news unless it's on *NBC News*"). For its loyal following, the CBS news program "60 Minutes" has for many years acquired such a status. "60 Minutes" is an investigatory format, wherein established CBS reporters inquire into a story involving a representative instance of some popular wrongdoing. A steady diet of this program might lead one to conclude that the world of power is unrelenting evil, from politicians to real estate dealers to doctors. The implicit attitude of "60 Minutes" stories is populist and romantic, wherein the powerful are constantly attempting to exploit ordinary folks. Although the intervention of "60 Minutes" has exposed this particular dastardly episode, the general assumption of the story line is that this is but one example of the ecology of popular wrongs that pervade society. "60 Minutes" is a prime show of what has been called television's "ironic model," in which reporter, format, and audience conspire to communicate a tone of "inside dope": this story demonstrates what lawyer, doctors, and developers are really up to. Audiences can share with the show a sense of disgusted superiority to such established felons but also a feeling of detached amusement. As critics of television have argued, a show such as "60 Minutes," and the many lesser tabloid TV news expose shows, may reinforce an attitude of entertained passivity, that the American social and political situation is hopeless, but not serious.[12]

These examples illustrate how different and familiar forms of popular discourse might be interpreted politically. Even though they may serve a mediating function for those who attend to them, popular discourses do not necessarily mandate a call for action. Rap music, gun and soldier magazines, and mainstream formats have an aspect of ritual play that in itself is satisfying to those drawn to them. A media constituency is temporary and mercurial, and does not translate easily into a political constituency. One of the mediating functions a form of popular discourse may serve is to speak to irrational urges deep in some personalities, and discontent latent in frustrated and neglected in marginal social groups, to the extent that they are deflected from political action. On the other hand, popular discourse may also energize potential political constituencies in search of articulation of their unformed images of the world. It may be too much to claim that *The Reader's Digest* created the conservative base for the rise of Reagan conservatism, but in its absence the popular mediating function it served for millions of like-minded folks would have likely been done by some other widely circulated magazine. As John Fiske has argued, such popular culture "texts" are not so much makers as "*provokers* of meaning and pleasure," both supportive and resistive to power. The structures of domination of a society may have an interest in exercising hegemonic power over "cultural commodities," but this must be complemented by the fact "of the meanings and pleasures available to the subordinate to express and promote their interests," including "the power to be different."[13]

But the politics of popular discourse includes not only the mediation of political structure (who has the power and who has not); it also includes the mediation of political time (what is changing and how that affects the array of power). This is essentially the mediation of political *fashion*, what is being thought, said, and assumed at a particular political time that adds up to the political *ethos* which pervades a popular society. Since in such a society popular discourse counts for something, it provides popular evidence of the times that are changing. The popular artists who implicitly and covertly (but rarely intentionally) interpret the present political time are exercising their function as the unacknowledged popular legislators of the world, affecting our image of politics and ourselves at that moment. Political fashionability is not frivolous, since it may reflect such life-and-death issues as an emerging popular mood for war and peace by "displacing" this concern into other settings. For example, the political fashion of the early 1950s was dominated by a fear of communism in the form of Soviet and Chinese aggression and subversion that might result in either annihilation through nuclear war or invasion and dehumanization, turning us into totalitarian robots. The wave of science-fiction films of the period represented these widespread popular fears by displacing the threat to outer space, where we were invaded and faced annihilation or dehumanization by suprahuman and ruthless beings (cf. *Invaders From Mars, Invasion of the Body Snatchers, The Day the Earth Stood Still, The War of the Worlds*) or subhuman and unnatural forces (*Them!*). The truly menacing political fashion of that day was almost too unbearable to face, so audiences could play with it only in a displaced setting which allowed them a way of envisioning covert political meanings and pleasures. Similarly, the news may sense and capture political fashion. During the pronounced Watergate scandal, it was the fashion for the national news media to investigate and criticize President Nixon, contributing to his political demise; but during the Iran-Contra scandal, it was not the proper fashion to do the same to President Reagan, simply because the *ethos* of the time was different, so he escaped enough press investigation and criticism to avoid impeachment. The news discourse of Nixon's time had different rules and limits than Reagan's time. How much of this was of elite or popular derivation is difficult to know, but the difference in mediation in news discourse had different political results.

Mediated Political Worlds

Many observers of the mass media are impressed with the extent to which the proliferation of the media has also pervaded our imaginative life. The argument is made that we have come to regard our own lives as less than "real" in the sense of not living up to the suprareality of the media. Nothing is deemed real in that way unless it appears a mass medium which can convey its reality to all of us who pay obeisance to media reality. In this view, media reality is more real than our own lives, tending us to think that what is true, beautiful, and good resides in a world beyond our own pathetic and imperfect existence. Popular media such as the movies and television become the latter-day manifestation of Plato's world of forms of which we are only shadowy and poorly wrought copies. Popular culture becomes the source of an induced inferiority complex to be overcome through hero worship of celebrities and pecuniary emulation through consumption.

In many ways this is the perspective of the media as *priest*. Media elites are the Platonic guardians of a superior world to which we ordinary mortals may only admire but not aspire. The producers and icons of popular culture are hegemonic justifiers of elite power to the many. But this must be complemented by, and even contradicted by, the view that the media are *bards*, the teller of popular stories and the transmitter of popular fashions. If the media are bards, then they also function as justifiers of popular power, the democracy of the common culture. Bards remind people of the legitimacy of popular expectations and the efficacy of popular experience. Media bards communicate folktales which are the common property of the many, turning into stories both the enduring and the fashionable meanings and pleasures people find worthwhile to heed. In this view, media reality is reflexive of our lives, tending us to think that the true, beautiful, and good resides in the world of our own existence.

In a media culture dominated by large organizations which control communication, it is easy to believe in the media as priest, propagating an elite-controlled reality that is perceptual and consensual, altogether what the media priests have dictated it to be. But the bardic function has never been totally undermined. For that reason, there is in our media culture a fundamental tension between priests and bards, stemming from our own popular ambivalence about politics. One of the continuous themes in both popular news and fictional storytelling is our widespread ambivalence about power. If priests remind us we are supposed to believe in elite power, bards remind us that we are supposed to distrust elite power and believe in popular power. Thus the media comes to represent a fundamental conflict in the popular mind, a conflict about our deepest beliefs and doubts about politics and government in particular, and all forms of power in general.

Long before the advent of the media culture, Americans had developed habits of ambivalence about authority and even achievement. As the media of the twentieth century recorded, the country underwent vast changes, changes that made political and social ambivalence all the more ingrained. Norms of equality and the experience of exploitation made the acquisition of material wealth suspect, while at the same time it was sought as the key to the American Dream. Thus in media depictions, there is an enduring tradition that wealth is somehow corrupting, while at the same time it is legitimate and rewarding to seek. The rich families of TV soaps (including *Dallas* and *Dynasty* in the 1980s) are beset by the burdens of wealth, while at the same time we enjoy their opulent misery we are envious of the very opulence which creates their misery. News brings us word of elite scandals, such as the savings and loan scandal, which reinforce our suspicion of the corruptibility of wealth. This at the same time we watch programs such as "Lifestyles of the Rich and Famous" and dream of winning state lotteries and magazine sweepstakes. Media bards (such as "60 Minutes") will also play to our sense that wealth is not a legitimate achievement that is ennobling and uncorrupting.

The same ambivalence exists in our forms of cultural expression, including our sense of the moral status of the country. Media priests such as *The Reader's Digest* tell us that a conservative moral consensus pervades the land, and that government should obey that moral law. But bards such as "60 Minutes" find moral corruption hidden behind moral claims. Tabloid TV and talk radio finds morality everywhere a smokescreen for perverse and selfish activities, usually criminal as well. TV soap operas find corruption in both bedrooms and boardrooms. On the other hand, situation comedies find virtue and community in the human comedy of ordinary life, although tinged with vulgarity, stupidity, and pettiness. But authority figures on such shows—military officers, lawyers, police commissioners, bankers, executives—are often portrayed as pompous, venal, and out of touch. Similarly, as mass media such as the movies and television become more varied and daring, our support for pluralistic and open cultural expression is put to the test, bringing ambivalence about our degree of tolerance. Media priests may urge elite hegemony over subversive expressions such as rap music or pornography, but the populace votes for such things with their channel changers and tape rentals. Just as with the power of wealth, we are ambivalent about the power of expressive individualism to fragment and change us in ways we are not sure are desirable.

Finally, we are ambivalent about civic individualism, in the ambitions and actions of those who govern us. Just as we worry about the benevolence and wisdom of the personal accumulation of great wealth, and the diversity of cultural expression, we also wonder about the politicians who rule us. We feel both great pride in our political institutions and values, and great distrust of politics and politicians. Media priests tend to focus on the politically powerfully, for both good or ill, since the elite perspective is that it is great men and women who are important in history. Even if those who become powerful are motivated by lust for power, and even come to a bad end, the institutional system is deemed so legitimate and effective as to insure systemic survival. Television miniseries which are biographies of eminent politicians will often display the not altogether admirable lives of the great, but affirm the continuation of the system. "The Kennedys of Massachusetts" portrayed the burning ambitions of Joseph P. Kennedy to both succeed in politics and make his son President; "The Final Days" depicted Richard Nixon in the last days and hours of his Presidency before his resignation. Even though the private warts and quirks of the mighty are shown, this is interspersed with their public acts within a constraining system. On the other hand, media bards may be more irreverent toward the mighty. Television comics from Johnny Carson to Jay Leno and print satirists such as Art Buchwald and Russell Baker make much fun of politicians, taking a more sardonic and even cynical view of the political system. So too may forms of popular expression such as rap music, which takes an alienated and contemptuous stance towards politics. These plural media expressions are indicative of popular ambivalence towards politics, which allows us to entertain at once the ideas that the American system is perfect and that politics is corrupt and cumbersome. In dramatizing for us both priestly and bardic perspectives on the world, the mass media serve a mediating function for fundamental tensions in our minds as to what the world is, and should be, like.

We began our inquiry in this second half of the book by noting that it may be presumptuous to assume that the mass media produces culture for the singular purpose of perpetuating a uniform ideology. Although there are media forces which buffet us both ways, the media influence us with tendencies toward diversity and even fragmentation as a culture as well as tendencies towards uniformity. Nor can we say the media are easily identifiable as conservative or liberal, supportive or subversive, narcotizing or invigorating. But we can say that the mass media have developed into pervasive and popular aesthetic experiences, so much so that many theaters of popular communication exist for us to enjoy, from which we may draw many different messages. Rather than perpetuating a hegemonic message through "consensus narratives" that brings unity out of diversity, in the late twentieth century the mass media dramatizes difference. This might help make us into a "nation of tribes" along racial, ethnic, class, or regional lines which correspond with taste communities for whom no single narrative or myth of consensus exists any longer. In that case, the mass media will have evolved into group medias which reject any single authority or story common to American culture as a whole. Then we will have to talk about American popular cultures specific to groups that identify with them, and abandon as lost the idea that culture is supportive of a united economy and polity. In political terms, the media of mass communication would in such circumstances play a truly transformative and revolutionary role, shaping the imaginations of groups to seek a new political identity. A new political world would then come into being, but the idea of the United States would be lost.

Chapter Seven
POLPROP: Popular Propaganda and Politics

In the previous chapter, we made the argument that the vast and encompassing media culture we have created is both influential and consequential. Politics occurs in its social context, and many of those who succeed politically (Ronald Reagan is only the most obvious) have become masters of media usage. Indeed, so too does economic and cultural activity.

Many companies and products who succeed in the contemporary world do so because of their media perspicacity, and many cultural creations, such as movies and toys, do so because of their ability to attract popular attention through the media. When we encounter such arts of suasion and persuasion, we are entering the world of *popular propaganda*. By popular propaganda, we mean largely mass-mediated communications directed at popular audiences which dramatize something to which its purveyors want to call attention and recommend an attitude and action. Popular economies, polities, and cultures could not continue without the great lubricant of propaganda to turn the wheels of commerce, politics, and culture. The related fields of advertising, promotion, and public relations have become major industries dedicated to understanding, shaping, and catering to popular desires and tastes. The "persuasion industry" is now a vast communicational undertaking, involving a great deal of money, organization, and talent with the purpose of propagating messages that sway us. We all like to feel we are immune from the impact of propaganda we are exposed to in our daily lives, but in fact we may not be aware of the impact of "hidden persuaders" and "subliminal seduction." In any case, it is not because the engineers of popular propaganda are not trying.

As with all mass media, we are again in the popular realm of extravagant expectations which our media experience can create and perpetuate. Such desire for entertaining persuasion and even

125

bamboozlement is a strain in American culture that predates the media revolution. At that juncture, some of the early geniuses of promotion began to refine the arts of seducing and shaping public desires. P.T. Barnum demonstrated that great masses of people responded to the most outrageous kinds of stunts and hoaxes if they are publicized properly. Early advertising pioneers, such as Albert D. Lasker, began to refine the "pitches" that attracted buyers for the burgeoning new products of the consumer economy. And practitioners of the arts of public relations, such as Ivy Lee and Edward Bernays, gave early shape to the "flack arts" of controlling and directing public opinion, in the practice of what is now called "spin control." In one way or another, such figures gave impetus to the spread of popular propaganda to the point that it is virtually a principle of our civilization, something that is so ubiquitous and obvious that we now take it for granted.[1]

In today's popular society, we may speak of the *logic of popular propaganda*. The practitioners of propaganda have legitimated propaganda to respond to messages skillfully designed to shape and direct our propensity to act. Propaganda logic dictates the efficacy of manipulation, appealing to common human desires through the use of popular art forms. Propagandists are adept at the use of dramatic arts, knowing what histrionic appeals to make to evoke emotion, thought, and action. What is called "hype" is in fact the clever promotion of a product, event (or pseudo-event), a personage or position. The job of the advertiser is to dramatize a product, of a promoter to dramatize an event, of a publicity agent to dramatize a personage, of a public relations spokesperson to dramatize the position of an organization. The "persuasion industry" uses the most sophisticated means—depth psychology, public opinion studies, social trend analysis, exquisite technology, even "subliminal" appeals—in order to propagate a message on which people can act. Propaganda dramatizes things to us which convinces at least some of us that we want what the propagandist tells us we want. All of us like to think that we are immune from the appeals of propaganda, but we all should ask ourselves from time to time why it is we think and do and prefer the way we do: is it our own free choice, or have we been persuaded, often without our conscious knowledge, through the adroit methods of propaganda? If we (for instance) wear fashionable clothes, is it because we want to, or because someone else has told us we want to?

If indeed propaganda works to the extent many believe it does, it then becomes a major source of popular learning.[2] We learn about ourselves, our culture, and our time from propaganda. Advertising, for example, is something we are constantly exposed to in our daily lives. From it, we learn what norms of self are deemed important, such as beauty, fashionability, and consumption. We learn what is important now in the popular culture—what stars, books, movies, and so on. And we learn from advertising not only that we should prefer this product, this movie, that star, but also that such preferences are legitimate and important. In other words, we learn from propaganda the legitimacy of propaganda itself as a source of learning, that it is all right to believe propaganda as a source. Propaganda propagates itself through convincing us of the efficacy of its message, legitimating it as a form of communication.[3]

The ubiquity of propaganda reminds us that public opinion, and popular choices, are not something which are left to chance. The logic of propaganda in a pluralistic society makes us into a vast popularity contest in which a variety of cultural objects and products compete for our attention and subscription. This has led to making extravagant claims for such propagandized things, raising our expectations as to what benefits they may bring. The claim that perfume brings sexual allure, or that a cassette course bring happiness and riches, or that a sporting event or movie will bring unequaled entertainment always finds takers, or more cynically, those who can be taken in. For propaganda to succeed on a wide scale, it requires the exercise of *popular gullibility*, the will of many of us to believe a communicator who appears credible. (The late movie producer, Joseph E. Levine, whose previews and promotions were always better than his schlock pictures, said, "You can fool all the people all the time if the advertising is right and the budget is big enough.") Once we suspend critical faculties, we may be willing to believe not only the logic but also the rhetoric of propaganda, finding the language of propaganda to be convincing and hopeful. In a broad sense, propagandists are always selling hope, the expectation that doing this or buying that will make our lives better.

Propaganda is a major source of learning because it is in large measure playful. When we watch a TV ad, or the previews at the movies, or even listen to a circus barker, we are playing with what they say. We are attracted to the message because it has an attractive dramatic structure with which we may play. A television spot ad for soap or perfume or whatever is a playlet that creates a fantasy around the product. We may learn about ideals of domestic cleanliness or erotic adventure with which we associate a brand of soap or perfume. The ad is thus not only a pitch for a particular brand, but also by inference for a way of life or pattern of behavior: cleanliness is a cultural norm by which you will be judged, and eroticism is a legitimate activity. Even though advertising involves vicarious play, it has an inadvertent impact on what we conceive as important and how we act accordingly. Since it shapes and enlarges our expectations, such propaganda may ultimately be frustrating, since it may create impossible ideals. If it does, then the play of propaganda becomes relevant for the society by affecting our political expectations.

Propaganda and Utilitarian Culture

Propaganda follows the money. It has long been evident that our economy, and the values that support it, have found propaganda indispensable. Economic institutions and wealthy families have found public relations specialists useful in shoring up their "image with the public." The Rockefellers hired Ivy Lee to revamp their public image after the Ludlow massacre, making the patriarch John D. Rockefeller into a kindly grandfather rather than the devil who ordered firing on strikers' families. Hollywood discovered very quickly that movies audiences were interested in both stories and stars, so the arts of promotion developed to hype movies and movie stars. The "search" for the fitting actress to play Scarlett O'Hara in *Gone With the Wind* was an elaborate hype to maintain interest in the long production of the film. The idea that a large part of the budget for the production of any good or service should be propaganda to maximize its consumption became an economic principle. Advertising meant that a better mousetrap would only sell if it had a better advertising campaign to publicize the product. It also meant that in a "consumer economy," consumption was limited only by the amount of debt that people were willing to incur. By the late twentieth century, propaganda had become the ultimate form of utilitarian communication, in that its utility was in furthering the goals of economic actors through the use of the intervention of promotion and publicity.

Propaganda is the language of a popular economy. Even though defenders of capitalism—themselves often propagandistic apologists—speak of a "market economy," "level playing field," and "the law of supply and demand," the intervention of propaganda narrows market choices to those with the means to advertise and promote, making for a highly unlevel playing field, and demonstrating that demand for things can be created and manipulated. But the use of propaganda also meant that the economic practice of giving people what they want becomes difficult to resist. Since much sophisticated propaganda is based on "market research," there are empirical means to not only know what people want now, but also what they can be induced to want in the future. We have thus moved from an economy of needs to an economy of wants, based on the legitimacy of ever-expanding popular consumption created by the manipulation of wants through propaganda. The logic of a popular economy dictates the primacy of both real and imagined wants, and of the "engineering of consent" to exercise those wants.

In order to shape and direct wants, the popular propagandists dramatized the legitimacy of desire in terms of cultural mythology. They may appeal to primal desires, social, or political desires, but the habit is to give them a mythic context. A perfume ad may appeal to the primal desire for sexual fulfillment, but will be couched in terms of the myth of cultural erotics, of what is acceptable at both an actual and fantastic level. Thus perfume ads suggest that smelling good becomes the catalyst for a drama of sexual adventure that leads not only to good sex but also perhaps a good "relationship." Ads for "natural" foods or the latest magic bullet— oat bran, wheat germ, garlic, or whatever—appeals to the primal fear of death, cast in terms of the myth of health, energy, and longevity and the social benefits (playing with your grandchildren) stemming from such foods. A soap ad may appeal to the social desire for acceptance, if your friends rave about your spotless glasses. And of course promotion and public relations will utilize such appeals—a movie preview may suggest sexual thrills and deathly frights, and PR people working for a corporation may portray it as benevolent, wise, and incapable of error.

It has often been argued that modern propaganda has had many detrimental effects. We have already noted that propaganda, in enriching our fantasy life, may feed our illusions and lessen our grip on reality. Activities such as public relations smack many as either phony or downright lying, making us cynical about what spokespersons, advertisers, promoters, and so on claim. But a major complaint goes to the heart of our material culture: advertising and other forms of propaganda helps feed greed and vanity, making us define ourselves and evaluate others in terms of the quality of our possessions. "Conspicuous consumption" can range from watches to cars to schools. Recently several elite private colleges have been accused of what is called "the Veblen ploy," raising tuition above $20,000 a year to foster the illusion that such academic conspicuous consumption guarantees excellence in the school and quality education for the student. Similarly, if we respond to the "snob appeal" for, say, a wine, even though that wine may be mass-produced and undistinguished, we feel we have acquired superior status. The desire for things becomes expansive, and we become consumed with consumption, believing that we are what we have.

Such an irrational pursuit of things has been called "commodity fetishism." Propaganda likely has given widespread credence to materialism as a widespread cultural activity, implicitly telling people it's all right to want things, and to shop till you drop. The American wealthy and upper middle class in particular seem to involve themselves in the relentless pursuit of things. A trip to any wealthy suburban house or urban townhouse will demonstrate how much people surround themselves with "status symbols," and evaluate people in blatantly materialistic terms. The accumulation of wealth functions to facilitate the accumulation of things. Material acquisition is seen as an outward and visible sign of an inward and spiritual quality, the power that let them make a lot money. In this popular logic, materialism and hedonism are deserved rewards for individual effort, since singular achievement serves the social utility of creating wealth.

Yet the valuation of the achievement ethic and material accumulation has social consequences that have eventual political ramifications. If income and consumption is concentrated in an exclusive class of rich consumers at the top, those with less will begin to feel relatively deprived. If great riches exist side by side with great poverty, then the potential for social conflict becomes greater. Too, if the logic of popular consumption as a deserved reward pervades as a social practice, then it will also motivate people with less wealth who can ill afford it. The result in the consumer culture of today is widespread and massive debt, with the sum total of personal debt exceeding even the public debt of the U.S. government! And, if people are bombarded with propaganda that tells them to have fun and spend money there will be less time for work; thus, time spent in play will exceed time spent in work, lessening the productivity and wealth of the nation! Finally, if the wealthy are obsessed with acquiring, they are less interested in work too, leaving a void in executive and investment leadership ranks, and in elite activities with social benefits such as philanthropy. The wealthy can in such circumstances become decadent, pursuing even exotic and exclusive activities that demonstrate to the have-nots of society their irresponsibility and unfitness to rule. From the studies of the impact of propaganda on children (such as we discussed in Chapter 6), it seems to be the case that the logic of popular consumption is learned at an early age, and that for some growing children (the so-called "yuppie puppies," for instance), consumption becomes a central preoccupation (to the extent that some young children can spell designer labels accurately, but not name the article of clothing it is on!).

It is clear that such a culture might valuate material prosperity so much that it becomes a catalyst for moral and political poverty. The obsession with material prosperity can make utilitarian individualism into widespread self-centeredness and selfishness, fulfilling Tocqueville's warning that a culture of excessive individualism can become incapable of moral and political concerns that make for community. If there is widespread popular consensus that it is every person for himself or herself, then the supremacy of private interests becomes paramount, to the exclusion of moral actions to ameliorate wrongs or public policy to insure justice. In such a society, both morality and politics may atrophy, since each individual is focused on his or her own individual interests. Marriage, for instance, thus becomes a temporary arrangement between two self-interested parties, a contractual agreement that is broken when one of the parties to the pact decides it is no longer in his or her interest. And politics is seen as just another area of social exploitation, with political leaders interested only in their own self-aggrandizement rather than the public good. Such a popular society of discreet and competing individuals might resemble a Hobbesian universe of the war of all against all.

Such a world would be created by propaganda which, explicitly or implicitly, extols the values which lead to the glorification of the individual at the expense of community. It is a question as to whether popular propaganda can overcome the excesses of individualism. There is plenty of propaganda that calls for altruism, voluntarism, and philanthropy, yet the amount of time and money devoted to social causes doesn't seem adequate to overcome growing poverty, homelessness, and poor health among a significant part of the American population. Nor do all of the exhortations to vote affect increasingly low turnouts in elections. Despite the deluge of official propaganda about the exercise of the rights of citizenship, an alienated or indifferent electorate finds little utility and no sense of community in voting. Popular propaganda may be able to lure the individual towards the pleasures of self-love, but not towards the pains of sacrifice and commitment.

Propaganda and Cultural Expectations

Even though the logic of popular enterprise has done much to destroy community (through development, mobility, suburbia, and so on), we may still say that there is a popular yearning to belong to some thing larger than oneself, if only at an illusory level. We are not willing to give up our often mad pursuit of wealth, power, and glory, but we do enjoy the illusions of popular identification. When Presidential politicians use the rhetoric of the American "city on the hill" or "family," they are speaking to the mythic obeisance we pay to the myth of community. But our commitment to expressive individualism at play, as well as utilitarian individualism at work, restricts our communal participation largely to the mythic. When we go out to play, we are largely on our own; fewer people affiliate with fraternal organizations; more people are childless or live alone. Further, we seek individual experience, even when it involves joining a group. Those who go on "designed experiences" (baseball fantasy camps, dream vacations, and so on) are seeking a unique experience.[4]

Propaganda not only underscores our cultural individualism, but also its popular fashionability. Our choices of popular culture are mercurial, since propagated messages may lure us away from one thing to do towards another. We feel relatively free to make such choices, feeling no loyalty to anything or anyone that is out of fashion. What we like and dislike becomes the major cultural arbiter of taste. Hollywood may spend many millions on a movie, but if the moviegoers don't like it, or find it to their taste, it dies at the box office. Propaganda can only convince us that it might be fun to try it.

The seeming paradox of American individualism is that it is commonly expressed in conformity to what others are thinking and doing. The utilitarian-achievement strain in us is rooted in the "inner-directed" tradition of our character, while the expressive-conformist strain in us is linked to our "other-directed" aspect. Even though we choose cultural choices as individuals, many of us choose to choose what other people (or "everybody") are choosing. Even as we exalt individualism, we practice forms of cultural conformity, in housing, styles, cars, and so on. But at the same time, we pride ourselves on our power of expressive choice, enjoying being at the leading edge of fashion, which brings about a new if temporary conformity!

It is a major task of cultural propaganda to appeal to these contradictory American impulses. For instance, consider the propaganda one receives when you apply to a college or university. Since the quest for students is highly competitive, institutions of higher learning have adopted the practice of making alluring appeals to gain students. Brochures and videotapes will typically stress that at Hooterville, you will find a plethora of cultural choices, and a faculty that is committed to academic choices that let you find what majors or courses are fashionable at the moment. Thus the school is not only a school, but also a place to have fun, do sports, and make friends, a place not only of career utility but also individual self-expression. Such a multiple image of the school is propagated for prospective students to foster the illusion that this particular school is distinctive and accessible, challenging but not formidable, play certainly as much as work.

Similarly, the American armed services uses this mix of appeals in order to lure recruits. The Army's "Be all you can be" ads are a clear appeal to individualism, both utilitarian (learn skills, begin your career you will finish as a civilian) and expressive (army training and life is fun, adventurous, and prestigious). There is no mention of civic duty, nor that one might actually have to fight in wars. At the time of the Iraqi conflict, it was found that out of every one hundred military recruits, only ten said they signed up "to serve their country," while 39 joined for college money, and 26 for a job and job training. They were also disproportionately lower-class blacks and lower-middle-class whites looking for some way out of poverty.[5] The recruits joined for a combination of utilitarian and expressive expectations, illusions dashed by the potential of being placed in harm's way. It is perhaps too much to expect that military propaganda designed to attract soldiers would stress the risks involved, but the portrait of military life painted for the soldiers-to-be certainly gives no clue that in reality real soldiers die in real wars.

As we have stressed, in the long run, propaganda can have consequences about how we think and feel to the point we take our cultural perspective for granted. Some of these consequences can be indirectly and subtly political. Propaganda can be an inadvertently innovative force, giving credence and impetus to cultural changes which have political impact. For example, feminist critics have correctly pointed out that much gender advertising portrays women in subservient and even demeaning roles and positions, making them the mere object of male gaze and transforming them into a thing valued for its beauty and deference. Yet that is not the whole story. For advertising, like all forms of propaganda, is basically expedient communication, using social trends and fashions to sell products; inadvertently, they may also implicitly sell new propositions. In the 1920s, ads directed at women took into account the new freedom of the "Jazz Age" by depicting and thus helping to legitimate women smoking in public. In the 1940s, many ads depicted women as serving their country in the workplace, symbolized by the wartime icon of "Rosie the Riveter." It has even been opined that the famous "Maidenform Bra" ads that ran through the 1950s and 1960s had a liberating effect, since they depicted women as asserting themselves both in public pride of being a woman and in public roles ("I dreamed I swayed the jury in my Maidenform Bra"). The Virginia Slim ads that began in the early 1970s associated the brand with fashionable modern women who were both feminine and feminist ("You've come a long way, baby"). Advertising propaganda through such depictions have subtly accorded a legitimate status to female utilitarian and expressive individualism, that it was all right for women to claim formerly male jobs and privileges. Although other propaganda emphasized feminine beauty and traditional roles, others gave credence to feminist goals, and still others maintained that "you can have it all." (The aforementioned Barbie ads include the gorgeous and fashionable Barbie in a variety of formerly male roles, including astronaut.) All this may create a great deal of ambivalence and role conflict in maturing young women, but it does suggest that propaganda is both sensitive to changing attitudes and the agent of changing attitudes without intending it.[6]

This should remind us that cultural myth is dynamic, and that exercising some kind of elite "cultural hegemony" over changing attitudes requires considerable popular negotiation. Maintaining a singular control over popular experience is difficult, and sometimes propaganda reveals that elite institutions and actors try to exploit and direct movements. With the annual celebration of "Earth Day" by the environmental movement, corporations and politicians jumped on the bandwagon with propaganda declaring that they too were environmentalists. Such self-declaration, critics charged, was lip service designed to deflect criticism at corporate pollution and government with polluters, developers and so forth, helping maintain political power in the wake of change in cultural attitudes towards the environment. Here propaganda may serve the hegemonic function of fostering popular illusions about the benevolence and concern of elites, when in fact it is a rhetorical dodge to avoid action on a problem of popular concern. In that case, propaganda serves the elite function of *popular deflection*, reassuring the populace that they share their values and are acting in their interests. If the world environment continues to deteriorate, it will be a question as to how effectively elite propaganda can continue to be in the wake of observable facts. Counter-propaganda by environmental groups might then become more effective, and a major threat to elite interests and cultural hegemony.

Propaganda, then, has a *polysemic* relationship with popular experience, propagating a multiplicity of meanings through the dialectic of initiating and responding to changing cultural attitudes. This is not to say that propaganda does not have great power to persuade, and that people cannot be bamboozled by the sophisticated lures of the professionals. But it is to say that the effects of propaganda are mediated, and mitigated, by popular respondents who do not fall over in rows to the appeals of propcomm.

Propaganda and Political Expectations

It can be argued that propaganda is the primary form of communication in contemporary mass-mediated politics. In a popular society, it is easier to sustain rule through propaganda than force or fraud. If people can be persuaded to comply, then rulers have a solid base of power in public opinion. For this reason, modern princes surround themselves with experts in understanding and shaping opinion, since favorable opinion is crucial to political survival and prosperity. These experts advise the political leader on how to shape and direct political expectations through the propagation of messages which the public deems credible. Like other propagandists, the political propagandist believes in the malleability of the propagandee. So the tendency has been in popular societies for politicians to rely on propaganda as a major way of exercising popular control. Since propaganda works best when it overcomes the will to disbelieve, it is most effective with the politically ignorant. There is considerable evidence that the ancient notions of the "citizen" and "the public" are actually confined to a relatively small part of the populace, and that most people are apathetic about politics, lack even the most rudimentary political knowledge, do not have an ideology in the forensic sense, have fleeting and often random opinions, and emotional responses to political events and personalities.[7] This is not to say that people are necessarily stupid, only that their ignorance makes them often pliant targets for the illusions and delusions of propaganda. Propaganda can only penetrate a populace that will respond irrationally, giving shape to hopes and fears associated with something political.

The most obvious and egregious form of political propaganda with which most people are vaguely familiar is the campaign commercial. Campaign propaganda has long extolled the virtues of the candidate, at least since Andrew Jackson portraying the candidate as a giant yet with humble beginnings, as someone with democratic roots yet with great accomplishments in fields other than politics. This form of popular identification combines in one personage the virtues of utilitarian achievement, living a popular lifestyle in an adoring family and stable community, yet notable for his (or her, increasingly) war record, sense of civic duty, and willingness to serve. A glance at campaign brochures from the most recent election will play upon those themes, constructing a pseudo-personality in which we are supposed to believe. Alternatively, candidates utilize campaign propaganda for character assassination of their opponent. This also in nothing new, but with TV spot ads, it takes on a new immediacy and viciousness that is difficult to counter. The opponent typically is stigmatized as devoid of civic virtue, and indeed is often associated with economic or moral misdeeds. The implication is that there is something wrong with him or her that is manifest in their conduct. In 1988, George Bush ads portrayed Michael Dukakis as so devoid of civic virtue he was somehow "against" schoolchildren reciting the Pledge of Allegiance (he had so vetoed such a bill in Massachusetts, since the Supreme Court had consistently ruled that such a bill violated religious freedom of students with religions which forbade flag saluting), and indeed had let murderers and rapists free on furloughs wherein at least one (a black man name Willie Horton) committed a crime. Bush defined himself by what he was not, as a patriot in favor of the Pledge and against murderers running free, unlike Dukakis. So stigmatized, Dukakis came to be seen as someone slightly foreign and illegitimate, not part of the populace with which Bush successfully identified himself (playing with his grandchildren at a picnic in one homey ad). The success of Bush's negative ads was such that many campaigns since have been virtual exchanges of negative ads accusing the other candidate of assorted infamies. These kind of personalized attacks appear to work with enough voters to sometimes make a difference, but they can backfire, or lead to lots of disgusted voters who just drop out and don't vote.

Another familiar setting for political dramatization through propaganda is the daily selling of the President from the White House communication staff. In their attempt to promote the public sense that the President is in command, doing the right thing, never resting, and in touch with the people, communicators constantly dramatize the boss. The Reagan "handlers" such as Michael Deaver were careful to stagemanage every public appearance of the President, attempting to control the Presidential image. The Reagans developed getting on and off their helicopter into high art. Indeed, Deaver was quite pleased when network news programs would run their staged images of Reagan going to and fro, looking Presidential, with the conviction that it didn't matter much what he said, or what the news reporters said about him, because what did matter was how he appeared. In a television age, propaganda is not just words, it is also the manipulation of appearances which override critical thought or expressions. Reagan made the public Presidency into a performance art.

The *propaganda of the performance* is not confined to the Presidency. In public settings, a successful performance can shape expectations through the adroit conduct of oneself in a mediated political drama. If public events are open to popular definition, then whomsoever can propagate a definition satisfying to the audience controls the media stage. The 1986 Iran-contra scandal was a case in point as to the power of an adroit performance in stealing the show. After much controversy and inquiry over the Reagan Administration's secret dealings, attention focused in Congressional hearings on Lt. Col. Oliver North, a national security functionary blamed for the illegal activities. The Administration may have seen North as a convenient "fall guy" who would assume blame for the decisions of higher officials (including the President), and the Congress saw him as a possessor of secrets which would reveal the secrets of, and deal a political blow to, the Administration. But North refused to sit still for a televised degradation ceremony in which he was the scapegoat. He appeared on TV, erect and proud, in Marine uniform, bedecked with his military ribbons. His discourse was defiant and cocksure, both as a soldier "only following orders" from his superiors but also one contemptuous of the assumed authority of the congressional committee. His performance was so impressive that he did indeed steal the show, becoming the hero rather than the villain or scapegoat of the play. Further, his very performance revived in Americans some very deep mythic feelings: the rectitude of a soldier sworn to duty, honor, country; that such patriotic fervor and bravery was not the mark of an evil man; that somehow he is of the country and not of the government. The propaganda of North's was such that he got the audience to identify with, and sympathize with, him. By affirming him, one also affirmed faith in the military, the country, and the values he seemed to embody. Just as Marilyn Monroe embodied innocent sensuality, or Lou Gehrig innocent sportsmanship, Oliver North embodied innocent patriotism. Like other such personages, our expectations of him likely proved to be extravagant; but for the moment of his performance, he was held in popular fancy. The fact that his performance was calculated and coached, and that he might have had the ulterior motive of seeking a patriotic last refuge from his accusers did not diminish his newfound standing with those who wished to believe in him through their scant knowledge of his propagated personage.

We may speak of the *performative event* as a medium of political propaganda. We have already spoken of the pseudo-event, such as a White House awards ceremony, staged for its propaganda effect. It is an event choreographed for the conduct of a political ritual designed to propagate a Presidential message. But other events, which have more "real" qualities, will also be conducted for their propaganda value. Military maneuvers, in, say, Central America, may actually exercise the threat of American military intervention, but at the moment "military theatrics" serve only a propaganda function: the U.S. invasion of Grenada in 1983 occurred in the wake of the Marine disaster in Lebanon, and after a long frustrating period of American non-intervention in hostile places like Iran and Afghanistan. Grenada was a convenient and likely preposterous target for American military intervention as a postage-stamp island in the Caribbean. But it offered Reagan a dramatic setting for the easy reassertion of American power, relegitimating the *idea* of intervention as beneficial and victorious. Thus the Grenada invasion was an exemplary act, proving that the U.S. was capable of successful intervention, even though this particular event was in itself of minuscule strategic value. An exemplary act is in that sense propaganda, as an example of what we were now willing to do again in more consequential places. A performative event like Grenada then acts as a propaganda precedent for more important interventions, such as "Operation Just Cause" in Panama in 1989 and "Desert Shield and Storm" in the Middle East in 1990-91. A performative event that precedes subsequent actions may convince many people that later and similar actions are both justified and easy. If so, it has served its propaganda purpose.

Indeed, we are now accustomed to the media practice of symbiotic cooperation with government propaganda agencies that communicates the image desired by officialdom. For now the primary discourse of established officialdom is propaganda, designed to propagate an official view of reality which is hoped to prevail. The Pentagon, for instance, is famous for couching the reality of military events in terms that either take the sting out of battle ("targets" become "ordinance configurations") or that war policy has resulted in another glorious victory. Vietnam, for example, was the "perfect war" from the point of view of official public relations; no matter what happened, it conformed with official expectations of progress towards victory. In retrospect, the official view was self-deluding, having little to do with actual events, but sustained the war effort until the bubble burst with the 1968 Tet offensive (which was also characterized as a great victory).[8]

Whatever its manifest content, the usual agenda of official propaganda is to persuade both press and populace of the essential civic heroism of a government agency as embodied by its representative. In the United States, we are used to seeing the President imagined for us as the representative of the government, and embodying the heroic qualities he is officially said to possess. The President is framed by his propagandists with a popular image, as a regular fellow concerned about many of the same things we are, and committed to the same values we are supposed to be. Much effort is expended to show the President as someone who likes what we like, and thus shares our enjoyment of cultural expression and indeed of bourgeois luxury. We do not begrudge Presidents riding in limousines as long as they profess to enjoy family picnics, country-and-western music, and other popular pastimes. White House propaganda teams understand the logic of popular identification through presidential recognition of the common culture. The cultural charm of the President is complemented by his commitment to benevolent ambition, which in official propaganda involves depicting him as engaged in personal struggle with opposing forces, foreign and domestic, but assuring us that his will to achievement will overcome on our behalf. Much effort was expended to depict President Bush as, variously, a regular guy who enjoyed high school football and disliked broccoli, that he was a tough guy who stood up for the flag and against America's enemies, and that at the same time he was man enough to want a kinder and gentler nation. Such an heroic mix is clearly propagated to shape popular expectations, but we may wonder as to the extent to which Presidents come to believe their own propaganda. We know enough from "kiss-and-tell" books (Reagan, for instance) to be sure that much of the image-building done by official propaganda is fraudulent. But propaganda often comes to be believed by the perpetuator as well as the target audience, and in so doing a political actor can begin to believe his or her own fraudulences. In other words, a President can be bamboozled into the extravagant expectations of himself being made on his behalf as propaganda to convince the many of his heroism. If a president does think of himself in terms of his contrived public image, he may believe that he has to live up to his own notices.

Indeed, creating a public image for oneself through propaganda may become something that has to be lived down. If facts disconfirm a propagated image, then one's carefully contrived reputation my collapse, as it did quickly with Richard Nixon and more slowly with Ronald Reagan. The same thing can happen to a governmental agency. The reputation of the Federal Bureau of Investigation, for instance, was developed under the tutelage of long-time director J. Edgar Hoover. Hoover cultivated the institutions of popular culture—movies, radio, TV, comics, books, toys, and so on—to utilize the FBI agent (the "G-man") as an official action detective who led the governmental fight against various forms of villainy, mainly spies and gangsters. This led to widespread public support for the FBI as an agent of civic rectitude, enforcing law and order on moral or material miscreants. But Hoover and his agency may have become a captive of the FBI myth also. Hoover jealously guarded the reputation of his beloved agency, and was reluctant for them to take on tasks that might undermine their image. It is said that in the 1960s, real FBI agents who hoped to be promoted to inspector had to resemble in style the actor who played Inspector Erskine on TV's *The FBI*. After Hoover's death, wrongdoing by the FBI helped to undermine their popular reputation, and they have never recovered their status in popular culture (no recent movies or TV shows with FBI agents as heroes).[9] Their difficulty now is that they had a popular reputation they could not possible sustain in the wake of actual performance and critical responses, so they have had to live down extravagant expectations initially built through popular propaganda.

Great Expectations

It may be argued that the major problem with much mass-mediated politics in contemporary America is that it is dominated by the logic, and language, of propaganda. It is true that the American populace is used to propaganda, responds to propaganda and even finds propaganda useful in making economic, cultural, and political choices. But we may wonder whether the "great expectations" created by propaganda eventually undermines itself.

Propaganda succeeds through the exorbitant claim which leads to the extravagant expectation, resulting oftentimes in excessive consequences, either through disappointment and disillusionment, or through blind faith in the face of disconfirming facts. In either case, the citizen is left with something other than what popular democracy is supposed to be, becoming either cynical and alienated or blindly loyal and mindlessly unreflective. Perhaps in the back of our minds we sense there is something wrong with propaganda, simply because it is a form of discourse that doesn't level with us. It is not so much that propaganda is a lie as much as that it's *phony*, giving credence to the fraudulent and misleading. Maybe we all have a sneaky suspicion that we are constantly being conned. Advertising may create great expectations that a product we buy cannot hope to meet, so we feel had. The videotapes and brochures from the college you attended on their basis was not at all as it was depicted in their propaganda, so you feel let down. The candidate we vote for because of his or her glowing and hopeful campaign commercials turns out to be a bill of goods. In such a propaganda-dominated world, we may come to believe that everything is phony and nothing is real and substantial. We come to expect products to be shoddy and disposable, schools to be concerned more with image than education, and candidates to be lighter than air. With our expectations dashed, we can discern no compelling reason to believe anything anybody says, nor believe that anything is less than phony. In that case, propaganda may have undermined its own logic by creating a world of skeptics. But it might also transform American consumer economics, higher education, and politics.

There is another possibility: propaganda will succeed in creating a nation of credulous believers, for whom the only choices perceived as relevant are choices between propaganda. In that case, we will live in a world of plural propagandas, but not rational choice. Popular propaganda would be the communications code by which we live, and through which we decide. But it would not be a code of critical evaluation. Rather it would be a language of phoniness, sustaining a phony economy, culture, and politics. The authentic would not be found because it would not be sought nor even recognized. In such a world, popular politics would meet only the expectations which the language of propaganda would define. Indeed, as social beings, we would only be what propaganda says we are.

Chapter Eight
SHOWBIZ: Show Business and Politics

The world of popular mass-mediation gave birth to what we know as show business. The logic of showmanship in order to attract and hold popular audiences necessitated appeal to the value of entertainment. As the mass media became prevalent, the ancient appeal of storytelling and tribal enactment was translated into sophisticated forms of mass entertainment. This appeal to entertainment value was to become a principle of media presentation, and indeed entertainment as a value was to become the "ritual center" of contemporary America.[1] By this we mean that many of us define what is important through rituals of play. Since play has become the center of self-definition, then what is learned through entertainment takes on increased value. Entertainment in such a society is not simply diversion; it is a mode of learning through ludenic representation. Thus the agents of entertainment, the artists and actors who create and communicate play, become central figures in a new popular culture devoted to the common enjoyments.

There were those besides P.T. Barnum who saw America becoming the greatest show on earth. A few observers who witnessed the meteoric rise of Hollywood as an institution and symbol began to see the new world of popular media. In 1922, pioneer movie director D.W. Griffith reflected on what the movies might mean. He thought that American heroism was changing: in the past, the national hero was likely to be the soldier; at the moment, he was the industrialist, or business tycoon; in the future, he thought, the hero would be the artist, such as the motion picture director or star.[2] Griffith undoubtedly saw himself in the heroic mold, yet his self-serving prognostication turned out to be quite prescient. For the age of mass communication has given great impetus to the art of communicating to vast throngs of people, and conversely, to the expectation of attractive communications among media audiences. The essence of communication arts is the power of attraction, making people pay attention to an attractive message. In a world of competing messages, those who possess the power of attraction become important figures we know and from whom we learn.

Show Biz and Cultural Learning

Show business offers us a dramatic and vicarious world of play, one that transports us to worlds of illusion and fantasy beyond the mundane barriers of our existence. Indeed, the very centers of show biz—"Hollywood," "Tin Pan Alley," "Broadway," "Nashville," "Las Vegas"—became symbols of the lure of fame, wealth, and glamour in a newly legitimated enterprise. Show biz represents our modern quest for notoriety, and indeed our virtual worship of those who became famous. Those who are famous show biz figures are rewarded with fabulous wealth. They live in palatial surroundings and pursue a glamorous play-life in the dream world we imagine for them. We think them gifted, different, and oftentimes, superior. They became a new class of conspicuous consumers whom we could only emulate in style, celebrate in admiration, or denigrate in revulsion.

For many Americans, the Hollywood stars were the ultimate set of ludenic heroes. From the start of moviemaking, both the allure and the price of the movie stars increased manyfold. They were a new aristocracy, the closest thing we had to native royalty. They were beautiful people, whose actions both on and off screen were larger than life. The stars led infinitely more interesting lives than we did, and thus were the subject of much mass-mediated scrutiny. They were both accessible and inaccessible, available for our media use as variously amusing, revolting, or desirable, and so on, but also living in a world and way beyond our reach. The lives of the stars were dramatic, a popular drama of vicarious play for the fan. The stars served important functions for the populace that followed their screen and off-screen activities. In that sense, not only the stories they enacted on screen, but their story as a star became a source of learning for their popular audiences.

The Hollywood stars are the classic example of the creation of a class of celebrities. Celebrities are personages who are celebrated in the mass media, attaining fame through popular interest generated in them, and losing it when they become anonymous again. A celebrity is in the prestige business, since he or she is someone who at the moment has been successful in being famous. They are famous because we have learned that they are famous, and when we no longer learn that, they are no longer famous and disappear. The celebrity depends for his or her existence as a popular personage on us acting as interested spectators of the celebrated and their world. Celebrities are symbolic figures for us, dramatizing values, styles, and actions we either admire or abhor, and representing symbols of importance to us. We measure ourselves by the celebrities we love and hate.

Our worship of celebrities is likely indicative of the deterioration of old faiths, such as democracy and traditional religions, and our need for the popular veneration of new gods. In a desacralized world, we find new figures with whom we attribute wonderful powers and qualities, even to the point of ascribing to them immortality. The saints of old are replaced by the gods of show biz, the immortal and ubiquitous Elvis, the beneficent ghost of Princess Grace, the brooding omnipresence of James Dean. Our devotion to celebrities is a kind of popular cult of personality, wherein we develop idolatrous expectations as to what they can do for us. Apparently many of us believe that fame is a kind of immortality, and by adoring those who are famous we too transcend the profane for the realm of the sacred. Modern media watchers have learned to follow the stars.[3]

We have watched the expansion of the entertainment industry, and the accompanying growth of celebrity stardom, with considerable ambivalence. Recall that in the nineteenth century, entertainment and those associated with it were thought to be disreputable, and in many places affected by the Puritan ethic such diversions as the theater or the circus was forbidden. But with the modern expansion of leisure time, discretionary income, and simply the desire to have a good time, entertainment became more legitimate and easily available. Popular entertainment also had its didactic function. The movies, for instance, became a way for immigrants to learn English and the myths and mores of American society, for urban migrants to learn about their new environment, and for both men and women to learn about new ways of acting toward one another. But the fact that the movies were proving to be a major new way of learning was upsetting to established elites and conservative groups, so there were attempts to shut down or control this new popular force. Yet there was something irresistible about the movies. For one thing, the advent and growth of Hollywood was a great capitalist story, in which utilitarian individuals (many of them poor Jewish immigrants) built Hollywood and great new sources of wealth. For another, there was simply the Tocquevillian principle of popularity: people liked to go to the movies, so it became difficult for political authorities to resist popular will. Yet despite the institutionalization of the movies, decades later they often remain controversial, and efforts are made to suppress films deemed morally or politically damaging.

There is also something irresistible about show biz stars. They are legitimated as modern exemplars of individual entrepreneurship, successfully marketing their popular personage as a commodity. Someone became a star through adroit self-promotion, one of the choice virtues of those Americans seeking their main chance. A show biz star was an instrument of fame, which led to the accumulation of fortune. In the American economic ethic, there was little that could be objected to in terms of achievement: even if a movie star was the object of popular fantasies (sexual, adventurous, or whatever), this was no more objectionable than, say, advertising. But again when the principle of the legitimate use of fame to achieve wealth is granted, this strains moral and political objectionability. Rock stars who base their popular appeal in the flaunting of propriety become difficult to stop. The logic of a popular society does not dictate quality of taste, and may include the celebration of the vulgar and base.

In some measure, many of the popular conflicts over the expression of cultural preferences involve the competing claims of utilitarian goals (selling expression, and maintaining that no one has the right to stop me from saying and selling) and "conservative" cultural standards. Those who sell and buy pornography and "splatter" movies, for instance, contend that no one has the right to set standards or define cultural limits. The expansion of freedom of expression at the expense of taste and limits has been facilitated by both the support and example of show biz stars. Hollywood movie stars did much to legitimate divorce and other personal activities (drinking), and their willingness to take their clothes off on camera and depict lovemaking likely also contributed to the loosening of sexual mores. If the stars of show biz act in any way as role models, then actions or styles depicted by them can become the models for their fans. On the other hand, show biz figures such as Ronald Reagan were quite capable of convincing people that they embraced conservative values as much as their followers. The difficulty is that those conservative values include the legitimacy of free trade, which for many suggests the logic of popular choice in cultural trade. So political conservatives among show biz folks can hardly espouse cultural censorship without undermining the very industry that made them rich and famous in the first place. There is clearly a potential conflict between conservative values and show biz values. When show biz people began to use their celebrity for political purposes, it followed that show biz values would be injected into politics. There was, of course, always an element of entertainment values in politics, such as the hoopla associated with conventions. Too, politicians had long sought the publicity that makes them celebrities. During the 1950s, the Kennedys of Massachusetts cultivated magazine exposure, making John F. Kennedy into a well-known celebrity. But when show biz figures began to advise, participate, and then get elected in politics, they thereby legitimated show biz as a source of political leadership and an entertaining style as a political virtue. The demand for things to be entertaining became essential in campaigns, Presidential rituals, and other highly public arenas of politics. As show biz and politics became more and more intertwined, the expectation of political entertainment became irresistible. A figure such as Reagan understood through career experience the uses of entertaining staging and rhetorical hyperbole for amusing political audiences.

The impulse toward political entertainment can be illustrated by the popularity of the "let's put on a show" ploy. When something is perceived as a public problem of crisis proportions—a disease, famine, poverty and debt—it often becomes the pretext for a show to raise money. In the 1980s, the expectation that the government would do anything about problems such as farm debt, Ethiopian famine, the AIDS epidemic and so on declined; and besides, the slow work of traditional charities was undramatic. So various concerts presided over by celebrities were held to both dramatize and raise funds for the problem. Political showmanship was deemed essential to the solution of a problem, although it was charged that putting on a show was a "feel-good" device to give people the illusion that the problem was now solved through ritual celebration. In any case, such staged events were an instance of civic individualism, a show biz enterprise directed at a public problem.

The Principle of Spectacle

The contemporary Presidential government in the United States rules through a combination of surveillance, secrecy, and spectacle. Like all governments, it maintains a system of surveillance in order to control populations and problems. Since drug use is seen as a threat to social order, the federal police apparatus coordinates efforts to impede drug traffic and use. The military and intelligence establishment utilizes secrecy in its various activities related to warfare and espionage. But for its public face, the Presidential government finds it prudent to use spectacle, events staged with show biz qualities and calculated for dramatic effect. Political spectacle for popular impression is as old as the pomp and circumstance of court, but in the mass-mediated age, it is organized and conducted by professionals from the world of show biz (including advertising and public relations, themselves branches of show biz). A spectacle is a show staged for a showbiz purpose, to showcase the appearance of benevolent and wise power. This has been called "the cinematographic model of publicness," with the spectacle serving as a political designed experience transforming the event into a performance and press and public into spectators.[4]

There are various uses for the principle of spectacle in popular politics. The political leader is prudent to make a spectacle of himself or herself, as a solid embodiment of political virtue. The Presidential appearance on the White House lawn, carefully separated from dissent or discord, is a spectacle to communicate the power of Presidential performance, commanding a scene choreographed for him by his managers. The public activities of the First Family (when possible) are designed to show a domestic spectacle of loving family and friends in the prototypical American family. A policy spectacle demonstrates government commitment to a program—drug abatement—through spectacular arrests, raids, and so forth, often staged because actual drug policy is not solving the problem. Similarly, a military spectacle may be staged as a "show of force" precisely because one may be powerless to affect events. In all cases, the event is a spectacle of power, designed to produce both awe and amusement by the ordinary mortals who watch it.

The use of spectacle enhances our expectations about politics by highlighting its entertainment value. We now expect to see, and be amused by, political spectacle, ranging from conventions to warfare. The party nominating convention used to be an event in which real political conflict occurred, with real debate and real competition for the nomination. But the focus of television and a mass audience brought into play the logic of popular media, and the convention was transformed into a media spectacular, usually tightly controlled and choreographed by media managers to maximize audience entertainment. Similarly, press access to military operations such as Grenada, Panama, and Desert Storm was tightly controlled in order to make the American conduct of warfare to look heroic and not horrible, as in the virtually uncensored coverage of Vietnam. If war can be communicated as a majestic spectacle, then it is likely to enjoy public support as a kind of cinemaphotogenic war, devoid of the horrors and confusions of actual combat. Grenada may serve as a model for a successful "media action" that conforms with popular cinematic expectations of the classical war film. Most of the post-mortem Vietnam films were filled with the horrors and absurdities of war, based in part on the coverage of that war. Beginning in the 1980s, there began to appear Hollywood films (*Top Gun, Navy Seals, Iron Eagle,* and so on) which extolled the martial virtues in the context of spectacular and successful combat, with a lot of soldierly camaraderie and high-tech gear. If the public support a new mood of national bellicosity, then the popular media may respond in years to come with stories of heroic warfare that make warfare seem fun again, a spectacle in which young people will want to take part. Such a change from the Vietnam era would signal the revival of patriotic militarism as the expression of civic individualism expected of vigorous and aggressive youth, wherein war would be its own moral equivalent.

Too, if we are in an age of the "imperial Presidency," the majesty of that office will have to be displayed in spectacles in order to sustain the illusion of political omnipotence. If we may use the "Rome analogy" (as many are doing as we approach millennium), it may be the case that the United States is in imperial decline. If so, the celebration of praetorian daring (as with Oliver North and fictional military and paramilitary figures) will be common, and the Presidential government that rules the "national security state" will find spectacle supportive of the military and the imperial leader to be useful. Like the emperors of the Augustan Age, as things become more out of American control, imperial spectacle is used to reassert the continued dominance of the emperor despite the accumulation of facts to the contrary. Since the imperial President symbolizes to the populace the majesty and power of the State, surrounding him or her with entertaining and awe-inspiring spectacle serves very real Machiavellian purposes. The "Liberty Weekend" display of 1986 (the centennial of the State of Liberty) was a patriotic extravaganza, with President Reagan presiding over an awesome if garish spectacle of celebration.

It may also become the case that as American society deteriorates, spectacle will replace efforts to reform social problems, deemed by both ruling elites and many voters as hopeless. The entertainment industry could serve as a medium of spectacular substitution, showing both the solution of problems (committed minority teacher transforming poor students as in the film *Stand and Deliver*) or the identification of new enemies (as in the anti-Islamic film, *Not Without My Daughter*). A problem such as drugs evokes the spectacular response of a "Just Say No" program, and pollution with a Presidential tree-planting program, both replete with the expression of Presidential concern and interest, visiting a drug facility or publicly planting a tree, while at the same time refusing to increase expenditures. Popular spectacle is satisfying in that it demonstrates that elites are "working" on a problem, since they are exhibited as being so. But if the mass media cooperate, the problem may be largely ignored since it is hidden from view, behind the spectacular facade which reassures and comforts us.

Similarly, entertainment spectacles have political uses in producing, and reforming, images of enemies. Hollywood and other popular media used to produce images of foreign and domestic Communists. With the changes in Soviet-American relations, the Russians tended to be transformed into likeable and understandable non-villains (as in the *The Russia House*), living in a romantic if still slightly odd land. However, a new foreign villain was needed with the eclipse of Russian culpability for world ills. In the 1990s, it appears that Moslem peoples might fill the bill (Latin American drug dealers might also serve). Moslem leaders such as Saddam Hussein, terrorists such as the shadowy nemesis of Oliver North, Abu Nadal, and indeed the entire Islamic world translate into excellent popular villains threatening us and our "way of life."

Thus the spectacle of fictional Moslem villains—Arab oil sheiks buying the country, terrorists attempting to blow up planes, evil dictators threatening Western women—become part of our vision of a new Them that has to be punished and destroyed.

In 1991, with the advent of "Desert Storm" in the Middle East, the possibility of a new kind of spectacle emerged. The uncensored spectacle of Vietnam on American television news had eroded support for the war and the military. Learning from that, the American military imposed tight censorship and guided information about the conduct of Desert Storm. The television networks very largely complied, transforming news about the war into virtual propaganda. This network-Pentagon cooperation suggested the advent of war as entertainment. With the use of sophisticated graphics, photography, and other visual technologies, television news was now able to attract a popular audience who followed the war story for its entertainment value. Since the censored news excluded upsetting images such as casualties and massacres, the war could be followed as almost a war movie, a simulated conflict devoid of the horrors of Vietnam. Obviously, many people were aware that what they were seeing was actual warfare, but the fact that the war was reported as spectacle gave it the status of a media appearance. Placed in a domestic and high-tech format, it held popular fascination as a newsworthy narrative because of its spectacular qualities. If war is made acceptable to media consumers by transforming it into entertainment, then it is likely we will see more military spectacles in future. We will also be seeing the ultimate fruition of the principle of popular spectacle.

Phony Politics

The infusion of show biz values and people into politics has given it a whole new aspect. Even though there has always been some entertainment value in politics, now politics as entertainment may well have become its primary function for significant sections of the populace. We may have transformed the citizen into the spectator, moving him and her from the role of a democratic participant to the status of a watching audience. Show biz in politics encourages a separation of the audience from the action, implying that they have no right to interfere with what goes on in the political drama. For example, celebrity sponsorship of charity shows suggests that little or no action is expected of ordinary mortals, since the stars have it in their power to sponsor the matter. Civic individualism thus becomes limited to the favored few who are part of the political celebrity network. A movie star has been President, and the Congress and state legislatures now have their share of former athletes, radio commentators, television celebrities, astronauts, former prisoners of war, and so forth. Nowadays when one achieves celebrity, or is noted for a new achievement, they are immediately mentioned as now "qualified" for public office. When celebrated pitcher Nolan Ryan achieved several notable baseball milestones, he was immediately thought in Texas political circles as material for public office. The emerging criterion for public office becomes more and more celebration rather than qualification.

In a mass-mediated age, with its insatiable popular thirst for entertainment, the reasons for this trend seem clear enough. But the triumph of entertainment value in politics is likely part of a larger trend, that of the United States as a phony culture. We now live in an immediate society with the emphasis on instant gratification and quick rewards. Our expectations are focused on the immediate, with little thought given to history and heritage as a guide nor future outcomes and consequences. Our desire for self-expression subverts much commitment to civic progress or even rudimentary civility with other people. Further, our desire for the immediate means that we focus on the pleasurable at the expense of the painful. We go into great debt to buy what we want now, and much of what we desire to buy are manufactured wants and contrived experiences. Like children, we easily fall into boredom and want to be constantly entertained. Time becomes the enemy, since it is the immediate that is to be enjoyed; thus time must be forgotten in an immediate experience that obliterates the temporal and all that it implies—aging, saving money, passing on a legacy to the future in a healthy economy, clean environment, and so on. Show biz provides us with the entertainment that fills our lives with the temporary happiness that we seek at the moment and for which we cannot wait.

Our obsession with show biz has helped make us into a leisure state, a society devoted to the pursuit of leisure at the expense of work and other socially responsible activities. Show biz taught us that the essence of life is to have fun. Much of what we call having a good time is organized for us in the various forms of show biz entertainment, from popular media to more exotic leisure such as "designed experiences" vacations to "fantasy island" spas and baseball camps. Time spent in the discipline of work is replaced by time spent in the leisure of play. While economists fret about the decline of productivity, early retirement, and alienation from the workplace, the show biz industry builds yet more gambling casinos, theme parks, and multiplex movie theaters. Indeed, the World Future Society even predicts that in the next century, robots will do so much of the country's work that people will receive a salary not for working but for playing, since there will be little menial work but there will be an entire entertainment industry to maintain![5]

Yet we should remember that show biz experiences are an artifice. They are designed and performed as artifices for our enjoyment. When politics becomes entertainment, it becomes essentially the erection and performance of artifices. Politics as popular theater may be enjoyable, but its reliance on histrionics as the basis of political communication means that it is phony. Presidential theater or other forms of political drama for popular amusement are not so much lies as they are fakes, "a matter not of falsity but of fakery."[6] The White House managers of Presidential artifice are skilled in the technique of media fakery, sustaining the illusion of Presidential greatness. The rhetorical style of Presidents such as Reagan and Bush is heavily flavored with hyperbole and self-justification, less interested in factual accuracy than placement in a symbolic drama of their making. Their confessions of "sincerity" and juxtaposition with media villains such as Khaddafi and Saddam Hussein seems more contrived to sustain the artifice of their personage than to communicate usable information or honest truth. As figures of political show biz, they are in the business of performance art.

The term "performance art" usually refers to those artists who make themselves part of their art through some kind of still or moving performance. But here we may expand this to include any cinematographic public performance which blends together elements of fiction and reality in an artifice of immediate entertainment. An MTV visual, for instance, is usually a pastiche of various elements blended together in a enjoyable unity. A Presidential appearance, such as disembarking from the helicopter and walking into the White House, is staged for media effect, and requires managerial attention to blend all of the elements correctly—

saluting the Marine, looking casual but confident, greeting the wife, petting the dog, greeting the crowd—all are now familiar aspects of a performative ritual designed to communicate the President in action. He is the real President, although the action is in fact a fiction. Reagan, with his acting background, set the standard for the performance artistry of Presidential publicness but Bush as well as Presidential candidates all cultivate the aesthetics of actor dominance of a scene.

Yet this is an emphasis on cosmetics that either substitutes or diverts focus on measurable and palpable problems. Show biz politics avoids evaluation in terms of instrumental solutions. Rather it excels at "symbolic politics," since symbolic enactments and representations are amenable to dramatization through performance art. A President doesn't want to be evaluated as an environmentalist by budgetary or other quantifiable measures, since he may in fact have cut the budget for tree-planting (as Bush did); rather he wants to be evaluated through staged "photo-ops" showing him planting a tree, and vowing to plant a billion trees in the next decade. This has been referred to as the *politics of simulation*, since it is an activity wherein the real is substituted by signs of the real.[7] Even something as extremely real as warfare can be made over into palatable media fare through the strict censorship of combat coverage, but also providing the media and public with interesting and sophisticated graphics and footage which make warfare seem like a video game. By selecting those portions of war reality which make it seem exciting, it is thereby placed within the fictionable bounds of war movies which gained Pentagon approval. The war happens, but what we see happening is a simulated reality bound together by the dramatic bonds of heroic and high-tech fiction. To the extent that political reality can be transformed into cinematographic fiction, it can be controlled by media managers skilled in the aesthetics of political simulation, making political reality into something that seems real but is actually phony.

The danger with phony politics is not only that it is misleading, but also that it is trivializing. The phony politics of Presidential simulations suggests that Presidents and their managers are focusing their attention and energy on cosmetics to the exclusion of pragmatics. They are not interested in reality-testing but rather fantasy-building, since after all they are likely to begin to believe their own propaganda and share in the illusions they propagate.

Politics at this level becomes a matter of manufacturing the phony, which deludes both actor and audience into believing that nothing in the world is unmanageable through proper Presidential performance art, and thus the problems or deprivations of the mass (health, wages, environment) are in a sense not real nor important. How far the Presidency can go through use of the politics of simulation appears to depend upon the extent of popular gullibility. In the Age of Show Biz, it may be the case that we expect from Presidential government not bread but circuses.

Conclusion

It has often been opined that the crucible of show biz, California, is the wave of the future in America. Politicians such as Reagan attacked the myth of the soft life that California seemed to represent for many, but did venerate the good life of opulence that Hollywood seemed to symbolize. Even though Reagan had in mind legitimating the good life offered by the acquisition of riches, it was hard to confine the desire for a good time to just millionaires. It is easy to convince ordinary people that the good life is the soft life, a life of play and not work, in pursuit of self-indulgence. In the "post-modern" world, the reigning *ethos* may well not be hustling to make good, but rather relaxing to feel good. In recent years, we have begun to speak of countries like the United States, or at least the "California culture" extant so many places, as a "culture of narcissism," in which more and more people are, like the celebrities they admire, in love with themselves, and willing to indulge the one they love. A culture of narcissism would indeed breed a society that demands immediate gratification, refuses to sacrifice, and is unable to take anything seriously or concentrate on anything very long. Such a culture makes for a mercurial and transitory politics, and certainly does not encourage governmental frugality nor calls for civil unity and purpose. The ultimate form of civic individualism would indeed be everyone doing their own thing.

There is another possibility stemming from the advent of a culture committed to the dominance of show biz values. Rather than becoming a culture of narcissism, it could become a culture of alienation. The phony politics of such a culture might just alienate people from caring about who rules them or how they are ruled. There is some evidence, based on studies of Americans, that the levels of cynicism, pessimism, and distrust of government have never been higher.[8] With the introduction of more and more show biz values and practices into politics, the result has been lower and lower turnout in elections. Perhaps doing your own thing by so many Americans is a result of realizing that what Presidents say and do for our consumption is patently phony. A phony political culture is one based in fakery, and may turn out to be as insubstantial as the blue smoke and mirror images that it conjures up.

Chapter Nine
FUTUREPOP: The Vision of the Future
in Popular Culture

The study of popular culture is not a precise science, and by necessity must involve us in speculation. We have to interpret what popular culture tells us about society and politics, and indeed we have to speculate about what popular culture tells us about the future. Since the future has not yet occurred, we cannot know for certain what it holds for us. But we can imagine it through the creative forecasting of popular culture. Let us here speculate on two trends or possibilities: first, on the internationalization of popular culture, and second, on potential political scenarios as envisioned by popular culture.

Cultural Diffusion and International Learning
The rise of the mass media and show business have made American popular culture the most popular in the world. Especially since the invention of television satellites, the ability of the mass media to proliferate messages and stories around the world has become phenomenal. People all over the world were able to watch coverage of the American war against Iraq as if it were a made-for-TV special. However, there have been vast changes in popular culture, to the extent that it is not now exclusively American, in either creative origin or corporate control. Indeed, in the next century we are likely to see a truly international popular culture bound together by mass-mediated networks and virtually independent of national control. We will have to try to calculate the political consequences of such a cultural network.

There was a time not so long ago when the world thought of popular culture as something created by Americans. The movies, for instance, became centered in Hollywood, and it was largely American mythology that it conveyed for the consumption of the world. Since the 1920s, much of the world's popular fare originated in the United States. Figures such as Charlie Chaplin and Greta Garbo were known in remote villages and towns in countries on all continents. Hollywood was a symbol of glittering allure to people around the world, who saw the American image of itself as it changed over the years. (It was not always a positive image—it was the young post-World War II French critics who noticed that many American movies were dark in mood and lighting, reflecting social gloom and pessimism, movies they called *film noir*.) In any case, what much of the world learned about the United States and the myth of America, it learned from the movies and subsequently from television. The ubiquity of American popular culture was yet more evidence of the pervasion of American power. Americans owned popular culture.

In the heyday of that ownership, Hollywood and other widely distributed forms of popular culture (music, for instance) were media of cultural diffusion. From the "entertainment capital of the world" came ideas and images which affected mass learning in the places where they were exhibited. It might even be argued that the "revolution of rising expectations" which agitated poor peoples in peasant and tribal societies was accelerated by the powerful force of the movies. The movies let people imagine worlds more opulent, educated, and urbane than the world of their immediate lives. In other words, their expectations were changed, often beyond their individual or political capacity to alter very much. If the poor or oppressed see a play-world of affluence, the question might occur as to why they don't have all that, and how can they go about getting it.

There is some evidence that something like this went on in eastern Europe. East Germans, for instance, could see Western German television, both programming and advertising which gave them a basis for comparison of their own lives with at least the image of life in the west. They may well have ignored ideological propaganda from the Voice of America, but they were very much interested in getting *Playboy* magazine, blue jeans, and rock albums. In many ways, the revolts in eastern Europe were fostered by students and other youths who were familiar with the liberating and rebellious messages of Western rock stars. Certainly then it was fitting that the fall of the Berlin Wall was celebrated by a gigantic rock concert featuring the international stars of rock culture.

It is likely, then, that the diffusion of popular culture around the world has important if mercurial and polysomic effects on the lives of people. Not everyone thinks that such popular diffusion is a good thing. A strict and ardent state religion such as Islam is at odds with the diffusion of Western popular culture, to the extent that American soldiers in Saudi Arabia were forbidden to consume much of the popular fare they were used to. When the Ayatollah Khomeni came to power in Iran, he purged the new Islamic state of all taints of Western culture, including rock music, which, he argued, was like opium in that it "stupefies persons listening to it and makes their brain inactive and frivolous." When China began to open its doors to the West in the 1970s, this included allowing in a great deal of popular fare, from cosmetics to skateboards to television and movies. But it may have been the case that this taste of Western popular culture fed the desire for more, leading to the student and professional-class revolt that so frightened the old leadership of the Chinese Communist Party that they crushed the rebellion, including shooting the students camped in Tianamen Square in Peking. But like eastern Europe, popular demand for such fare becomes difficult for a regime to refuse. As far as China goes, the old guard must be asking itself, how are you going to keep them down on the (collective) farm after they've seen TV?

It is also argued that the diffusion of popular culture is a manifestation of American cultural imperialism. Like other local industries, countries will often try to limit the amount and type of American popular culture they will allow in. This may often be done out of economic as well as cultural motives, since they may not want to "Americanize" the country. A corollary argument is that the subtle message imbedded in American popular culture is the celebration of American power. There is no doubt that some artifacts of American popular culture—some war films, *The Reader's Digest*, perhaps even the classical Western—are supportive of the more aggressive forms of American power. This view is complicated by the fact that a good bit of American-produced popular culture is critical of American, and often, of organized power itself.[1]

Indeed, it is probably fair to say that the old model of cultural diffusion is inadequate and outmoded. In the United States, there is more cultural infusion than ever, as European rock and Latin American movies and Chinese goods are imported. But more importantly, popular culture is no longer in any meaningful sense American. The internationalization of popular culture is such that it is just accidental that Hollywood is in the United States. Japanese investors have long since bought up controlling interest in movie studios and other large organizations of mass communications. This does not mean that they will "Japan-ize" the content of American movies, but it does probably mean that American films will be more attuned to international markets. What we are witnessing in the late twentieth century is nothing less than *the internationalization of popular culture*. This means that corporate control of such popular culture as movies, music, books, and so on will extend worldwide, and will take into account marketing on a worldwide basis. If there ever was exclusive American hegemony over the cultural message of popular fare, that is likely now past.

This internationalization of popular culture is part of a growing world culture. Popular culture may act as a kind of pop esperanto in the growth of a common culture shared in many areas of the world by providing a kind of common language which people of very different cultures can share. This might include sporting events such as the World Cup or World Series (including baseball teams from Japan and Latin America). Now there are film festivals all over the world wherein movies from a wide variety of countries are viewed. So there is much that can be shared together. But it remains to be seen how much international understanding is promoted by the internationalization of popular culture. In some places, it may seem to be an alien force and will be resisted, either by the authorities who are afraid of its liberating influence, or by traditional masses, afraid of its threat to established beliefs and ways of life.

If popular culture does create a "global village," it will likely be carried by the youth culture that has the opportunity to travel and share popular culture abroad. Such youths are likely the elite-to-be in various countries, so to the extent they share with other youths a common language of popular culture, they may realize that the world has something in common. If young Americans, Russians, and Chinese share fashion, music, books, and so on, they will come to power someday with a shared perspective denied to their predecessors. However, we should not wax too sanguine about the pacific implications of international contacts and shared culture. After all, Europe in the years before 1914 experienced a good deal of open travel, contacts by young people from various countries, and much common culture; yet during World War I, these selfsame youths were killing each other on the Western front.

There is another dark possibility we must point out. International corporate control over popular culture may not mean more advanced diffusion, but rather tighter scrutiny and exclusion of popular expression. Since "multi-nationals," such as book companies, have to operate all over the world, they may refuse to publish controversial books that will upset a local market or culture (such as Salman Rushdie's *The Satanic Verses*, which upset the Islamic faithful). Further, since such large corporations are exemplars of capitalist organization, they may be loath to publish books critical of capitalism. They might give priority to books which are essentially propaganda. Thus rather than enhancing the growth of a free and critical popular culture, they could wind up inhibiting or misusing the power they hold over communication.

Yet it may be the case that there is something irresistible about what we might call the "popularization of the world." It is difficult for even international corporations to inhibit the flow of communication if people demand it. In virtually every corner of the globe, there is great popular demand for a better life, which includes more access to popular culture. The desire for material betterment is accompanied by a desire for experiencing wider and richer forms of expression. People not only want prosperity and political participation, they also want access to an expressive culture. Indeed, it may even be the case that in many "Third World" countries, creating prosperity is not feasible and allowing political participation is considered dangerous, so governments will instead attempt to provide popular culture as a kind of opiate of the masses. In other words, *barrios* and slums around the world may have populations who are poor and powerless, but do have access to television, music, and other forms of entertainment that take their minds off their hopeless plight.

On the other hand, the proliferation of international popular culture might have the effect of creating a new mythology not tied to a national state. A new popular myth not tied to specific national or ideological interests could become a powerful force in the world, and would be amenable to manipulation. The centers of mass communication could produce fictional heroes with whom the great world populaces identify, but who might serve corporate interests through advocating deference to authority. On the other hand, a new myth is difficult to control if it is a compelling and hopeful narrative, so international popular heroes might emerge to act out the myth. These new heroes would obviously have to embody this new mythic power, and thus have to speak an international language and represent international hopes and fears. If it is the case that music is the international language, then it might be that musical stars might become a potent political force in such a world. If television can reach into a vast array of places, musical stars might be able to articulate a new international myth as no one else could. Such a new hero might serve corporate interests as a public spokesperson for elites attempting to quell worldwide mass restlessness. On the other hand, a new hero could represent a movement which aims at promoting international peace and environmentalism. In any case, the "wired" world in which we will live will be one in which the opportunity for new popular leadership unprecedented in history could arise.

Technofables

Indeed, in many contemporary futuristic tales, the inadequacy of old myths and political arrangements is a constant theme. Since we live now near a millennium, there is a real apocalyptic sense at the moment that the world is close to enormous changes. War in the Middle East revived ancient images of Armageddon, while more secular futurists warned of nuclear war, environmental disaster, overpopulation, and the breakdown of civilization. Others by contrast envisioned a Utopian future of peace and prosperity brought about through technology. Indeed, a good bit of popular culture which attempted to envision the future involved an attitude toward technology. This is why we term such tales *technofables*, since they revolve around the ability of technology to create material, moral, and political prosperity or poverty.

Indeed, one major strain in contemporary popular culture is patently anti-technological and in a sense is a yearning for a kind of pre-modern archaism. Yet too these tales are often projected into the future in a fantasy of post-civilizational life, often after a nuclear holocaust or breakdown of civilization. Such tales involve Gothic primitivism, with violent clashes of warriors struggling for survival in a barbarian world devoid of material wealth or any moral bounds save personal codes of chivalry. Such folktales are deeply rooted in a youthful desire for adventure, for the triumph of good over evil, and for the reappearance of magical powers in the world. From Tolkien to Conan the Barbarian to Dungeons and Dragons, there is much play with a past and future Dark Age of heroic clashes and beautiful princesses and evil tyrants. As a matter of fact, it has been feasible to combine such a mythic past with an imagined future, most notably in the *Star Wars* cycle, wherein space technology is combined with archaic features such as a samurai order, mysterious lands and strange peoples, and evil tyrants. The expectation lurking in such tales is one of a future of primitive violence and values, even if accompanied by the use of futuristic technology. And indeed, future wars, such as the Mideast war of 1991, may well resemble this, combining ancient hatreds with "state of the art" military hardware.

It is striking to see how much play there is as we near the millennium with the breakdown of civilization, what we might term the *Mad Maxian* scenario. A trip to any tape store reveals the vast array of post-civilizational movies in the "Road Warrior" vein, depicting a future of an urban or "outback" desert, with all semblances of civilization gone. The urban wasteland of New York (as in *Escape from New York*) or Los Angeles (as in *Blade Runner*), the huddled post-apocalypse enclaves of *The Terminator*, the decayed "New Detroit" of *Robocop*, all encompass an "urban Gothic" image of the future in which peace and prosperity are gone. The many "warriors of the wasteland" films imagine a future struggle for marginal survival of a depleted human race fighting amongst themselves in vandalous gangs and tribes for the few scarce resources left. The self-destructive savagery of the old civilization is now replaced by an even more primitive savagery in the struggle for survival amongst the ruins of a civilization which had destroyed itself. (Indeed, in the popular television series *Beauty and the Beast*, a civilized medieval order exists beneath the streets of New York, while the life of the city above is a savage jungle of gangs, greed, pollution, and violence.)

The *Mad Maxian* scenario envisions a future of chaos, created by the technological danger of nuclear war. Recurrently there are popular technofables about the conduct of nuclear war. The made-for-TV movie *The Day After* gave us a horrifying glimpse as to what the world would look like in the immediate aftermath of nuclear war. The movie *Wargames* offered a fantasy about a

Sorcerer's Apprentice who stops a Frankensteinian creation—a wargaming computer—from beginning World War III. In both cases, the story was about technology out of control, speaking to the fear that the existence of complex technology that guides warfare will bring disaster on without humans being able to stop it. Such popular artifacts remind us of the Faustian bargain of nuclear weapons, and how we may be ultimately defeated by our own mad creations.

However, much futuristic fare deals with the conflict of malevolent and benevolent empires, usually in space wars pitting high technology against each other in often violent conflicts. The *Star Wars* technofable featured dazzling space wars against the evil Empire by a democratic if equally violence-prone alliance. The new *Star Trek* still has its "prime imperative" of non-intervention in the new life forms it seeks out, but it is clearly an imperial vessel representing a federation of powers interested in the defense of territory and the exploitation of resources in an empire that is both defended and extended. Even though the ostensible role of the *Enterprise* is conflict resolution, the ship of state encounters quite a few hostile powers, with which it is often willing to take action. Thus the *Star Trek* political enterprise legitimates the role of a benevolent, if self-appointed, empire to police the political galaxy. This task is envisioned as a transcendent adventure undertaken with a high degree of moral rectitude, pitted against non-human peoples who might be our equal in technology but not in moral purpose and political values. *Star Trek* offers us a parallel universe to the politics of Earth, in which a united federation of states, led by the United States, takes actions against hostile states (such as Iraq) who are regarded as lacking in morality and political wisdom, so much so that that justifies violence to preserve and extend the interests and values of the coalition (oil). *Star Trek* exemplifies the kind of imperial conduct one might associate with the management of a New World Order.

One of the older traditions in science fiction and futuristic writing was the imagination of Utopian worlds, freed of power and ruled by science which brings inevitable progress. Utopian writers tended to believe that politics was bad, but that the rule of science in planned communities, such as imagined by Edward Bellamy in *Looking Backwards*, could achieve a state of social and political perfection. But such visions have fallen on hard times as science became more the faustian midwife of chaotic imperfections such as war and mass destruction. Nevertheless, the ideal survives, at least in popular form, in Walt Disney's Florida vision of a futuristic "high-tech" community as modeled in his Epcot Center. In fact, such an ideal is extant in such planned communities as golf retirement communities, Christian villages, pleasuredome penthouses, and the like. Such visions are exclusionary, often "high consumption" ways of life open only to a wealthy few, and have virtually disappeared as an ideal from futuristic visions in science fiction.

However, "low-tech" visions abound. Doubts about the benevolence of technology have developed since the application of technological innovation in warfare, demonstrating that new technologies are twisted into instruments of death. What has emerged instead are images of a low-tech world that is harmonious with nature using technologies as instruments of life. These "green" utopias imagine a material community based on cooperative rather than competitive principles, an egalitarian and libertarian culture, and helpful and tolerant politics. The success of Ernest Callenbach's novel *Ecotopia* in inspiring environmentalists and European "Green" parties shows the appeal of such a world.[2] Callenbach imagines a future state comprised of northern California, Oregon, and Washington, having seceded from the hopelessly polluted United States. *Ecotopia* becomes an ecologically-balanced, "human scale" society with humane technologies and politics, a model that many people find appealing. Indeed, *Ecotopia* is one of the few hopeful visions of the future around these days, an indication of growing pessimism about the future.

The Dystopian Technofable

The political experience of the twentieth century gave credence to negative visions of the future. These imaginings did not see a future of chaos, but rather one of control. For modernity did bring with it a "control revolution," the increasing ability of elites to use techniques of control. The technology of surveillance alone has advanced to the point of keeping close track on the movements of millions of suspect people, including telephone calls, TV choices, and conversations. But what worries the dystopian futurists is that every technological innovation, from computers to psychological "behavior modification" techniques, has the potential to be put

to use in controlling populations. Such futures usually take two
forms: rule through a technology of pain, and rule through a
technology of pleasure. These constitute two distinct dystopian
traditions.

The tradition of the technology of pain we may term *Orwellian*
after George Orwell, the prophet of the brutal nature of modern
totalitarianism. Totalitarianism in Stalinist Russia and Nazi
Germany pioneered the technique of using fear, intimidation,
torture and death as instruments to expand rule. Orwell foresaw
that such rule, if carried to its logical perfection, would transform
society into a huge concentration camp. His novel *1984*, satire
Animal Farm, and essays altogether offer a portrait of a future
Superstate armed with advance technologies of pain, exercising
about as absolute rule as can possibly be imagined. Surveillance,
for example, is advanced to the point of "telescreens" (what we
now call interactive television) everywhere as the ubiquitous and
inquisitive eye of the State. Every act, every utterance, even every
thought is suspect; one cannot trust anyone, including oneself, since
you might commit "thoughtcrime." The State rules through a
combination of external suppression and internal repression. One's
energies are supposed to be directed toward work and service for
the mythical symbol of the State, "Big Brother." Thus, sex is
discouraged, and young women unite in their political chastity in
the "Junior Anti-sex League." The family is to be eliminated, as
are emotional ties between people, as well as sexual feelings and
even the physical orgasm. The idea that sex is satisfying and love
is possible is denied and made a crime.

Orwell's picture of a totalitarian future is still horrifying to
us, perhaps because we sense that much of what he predicted is
still possible. In such a world, individualism is non-existent, and
the idea of utilitarian self-interest, free expression, or civic
participation actual crimes. But the interplay of fact and fiction
in science fiction reminds us that totalitarian states attempted to
realize such rule, and that in the future advances in the technology
of control may make such a State at last feasible. Indeed, one futurist
has predicted that the future will be characterized by "'survival states'
which blend a 'religious' orientation with a 'military' discipline."[3]
Such states are a result of military, economic, or environmental
chaos, surviving through strict controls on individual choice.
Political survival necessitates ideological conformity and

enthusiasm, with society mobilized and regimented into paramilitary organizations which can enforce discipline and administer scarcity. But as Orwell foresaw, the difficulty in such states is that power becomes an end in itself, measured by the extent and depth of its control over mass behavior.[4]

Clearly in the Orwellian tradition is Margaret Atwood's novel *The Handmaid's Tale*, which imagines an immediate American variant. In the wake of AIDS, pollution, and the breakdown of the family, America comes to be ruled by a quasi-religious order of men that enforce a regimented caste system in which one female caste, the "Handmaids," are designated to procreate to perpetuate the elite ministers and offset the drastic decline in population. The "Republic of Gilead" is ruled by a ministerial elite whose religious orientation give them ideological justification, organizing society into quasi-military organizations with medieval touches. *The Handmaid's Tale* suggests that fundamentalist Christianity, just like fundamentalist Islam, might be the framework for an Orwellian world ruled by the technology of pain.[5]

The imagination of a future technology of pleasure we may term *Huxleyian* after Aldous Huxley, whose novel *Brave New World* offered a more long-term and "scientific" version of what might befall us. The technology of pleasure is administered by a benevolent elite who create a world of shallow uniformity. Everyone has been psychologically conditioned since birth to believe that they are happy because they are well-adjusted. Society is organized into a functional class system, wherein everyone is scientifically assigned to a place in the scheme of things. Drugs are widely used to suppress pain, stimulate pleasure, and avoid thought. Eugenics are used to produce the requisite human types manipulable by society's scientific managers. Children are produced in laboratories, the family is forbidden, and sexual promiscuity is widely permitted in controlled situations. Everyone is taught comforting slogans that reinforce behavioral patterns ("You can't consume much if you sit still and read books"). This is a technology of pleasure in that social control is exercised without recourse to brutal power or direct suppression, with a velvet glove rather than a mailed fist. Huxley's future dystopia is clean, efficient, and orderly, but it is also inhuman. It uses the most advanced technological means to create a world of cheerful robots devoid of any human depth. People here are not forced into servitude; rather they are persuaded that they are happy, and willingly accept their servitude. Orwell's dystopia is sinister; Huxley's is just silly. The difference may be that a sinister regime resembling Orwell's world collapses of its own malevolence; but a regime such as Huxley's might go on because it demands little from its subjects while providing them with paltry pleasures and irresponsible joys.

Some have suggested that the future of the United States might resemble Huxley's world more than Orwell's. It might be the case that our culture will become more frivolous than malevolent. We are already heavily conditioned by advertising to consume, taught to believe in preposterous slogans ("It's morning in America," "A thousand points of light"), and told to not worry, and be happy. We are a society devoted only to our paltry pleasures, and avoid sacrifice or commitment. We spend much of our time consuming, but none contemplating the consequences of that consumption. Americans have built an immediate society, one that lives for the pleasurable moment, living only for its own selfish frivolity. The technology of pleasure that brings us popular culture has turned us into spoiled children, devoid of responsibility or even competence, happy only with the designed experiences with which we fill our time. If this is what we are becoming, then Huxley's world is much with us.

Conclusion

The older success of Utopian literature was because it spoke to popular hopes; the newer success of Dystopian literature was because it spoke to popular fears. It is likely the case in the late twentieth century that we find the future more fearful than hopeful. There is good reason for this, as the futurists daily issue dire predictions about such phenomena as desertification, the greenhouse effect, the disappearance of the world's flora and fauna, overpopulation, and so on. If we see a future of either chaos or control, then there is not much to hope for. But the success of the ecotopian vision does indicate that there is popular sentiment for some hopeful visions of the future. Perhaps we shall soon see a revival of utopian works with popular appeal, which can engender hopes absent in the bleak present. If we can imagine disaster, we can also imagine ways and means to avert disaster. If we defeat the worst impulses of politics, and the misuses of technology, it will be in part because we constructed futuristic fables that helped us imagine why and how we might do so.

Conclusion:
Popular Culture and the Twenty-First Century

The bleakness of much futuristic imagery at the turn of the century reminds us of the importance of popular culture in giving life to our world-view, including the future. Indeed, the Persian Gulf war of the 1990s aroused again the debate over the role of popular culture in our society: are we violence-prone and war-like because from childhood on we learn from popular culture the virtues of violence and the bold adventure of warfare? We argue over popular culture because we know it to be important, helping to define what kind of society we think we are and would like to be. Since we are now facing a new millennium, it behooves us to consider the popular culture that might emerge in the new century.

The Demonic Monomyth

New millennia are often new beginnings, so it may be the case that the twenty-first century augurs significant changes in our lives. The futuristic literature we just discussed gives us a clue that the world of the future might not be the same as it ever was. Now intellectuals talk about the "post-modern world," attempting to delineate what is happening that is going to make things not the same as they ever were. No one quite knows what the post-modern world is before or "pre-," but there is a widespread feeling that we may be on the verge of something momentous. The world of 2050, which many readers of this book will live to see, will likely be very different from the world of 1950 or even 2001. Our stories, and therefore our sense of self and society, could derive from a new myth.

We have already suggested several aspects of popular politics and society that might persist into the future—propaganda, news as entertainment, show biz values, even the advent of dystopias. But popular communications with political impact will only be effective if it is thought legitimate, in the sense of having symbolic

171

meaning for large numbers of people. If the post-modernists are right, it may be the case that we are living in a "liminal," or in-between age, in which old myths are being replaced by new realities and thus new myths. New myths may in fact resemble the old ones, but humankind's search for political and social meaning will determine us to seek for a mythology suitable for the twenty-first century. If it is the case that our extravagant expectations are now declining and becoming pessimistic, this may signal a coming crisis of belief.

If a society's beliefs are dramatized in its popular myths, then disbelief in those stories as equipment for living becomes critical. For if people drift through life no longer willing and able to believe in the established myth of God and country, then they may experience anomie as the myths atrophy in social function. If Christianity and American nationalism are becoming part of our declining expectations, they may be disbelieved. On the other hand, as they are increasingly disbelieved by some, they may be all the more ardently defended by others. One of the demonic potentials we might face as Americans is an attempt to enforce public belief in old myths as a test of orthodoxy, which makes us well on the way to enacting a dystopian political drama.

In the wake of rapid and destabilizing change, we might be tempted by the *demonic monomyth*. As defined by Jewett and Lawrence, the American monomyth took on a definite pattern familiar to heroic cycles worldwide: a hero hears the call of the community, emerges from humble or obscure circumstances to act for the community, takes the risks and is tested, journeys to meet his or her destiny, and triumphs over the enemies of the community.[1] In the United States, political heroes cast themselves in these familiar heroic terms, offering themselves as redeemers of the community. In our history, we have witnessed different types of political redeemers. Some are called "Heidi redeemers," appealing to moral transformation, such as Woodrow Wilson or Jimmy Carter; others are royal redeemers, such as Franklin Roosevelt or Ronald Reagan (drawn from the celebrity royalty of Hollywood); and still others are technocratic redeemers, offering redemption through technical mastery, such as Herbert Hoover or erstwhile managerial candidates, such as Jerry Brown or Mike Dukakis. All these types are within the usual political bounds. But there is a fourth type, the demonic redeemer. In periods of crisis, people often want a hero who is more elemental, vindictive, and aggressive. If a community desires to lash out at a world that they believe has betrayed them they find a leader who can identify popular rages and find popular scapegoats on whom to blame our ills. Like Captain Ahab of Melville's *Moby Dick*, such a figure could lead us on a demonic quest, a quest in which we abandon all of our inherited values for vengeance and destruction. Both Vietnam and the Gulf war demonstrated our capacity for violence; as economic power and initiative passes elsewhere, and the American moment seems to be passing, we might harness that capacity against domestic rather than foreign devils.[2]

A demonic redeemer may not seem to us to do evil, but evil is as evil does. Such a figure would likely be familiar and even folksy, but would be a charismatic personification of the fanatical will to believe in the validity and vitality of enforced national myths. Such a movement would assert the power of such a personage to work political magic in making the world and our place in it the same as it ever was. The more that the world resists our will, the more we would become willing to abandon civility and democratic constraints. At that point, politics has become demonic, with a nation possessed of an evil spirit, willing to invoke what the Old Testament Hebrews called "the lawless." In such a demonic quest, we may well burn the American village in order to save it.

The epic drama of the demonic monomyth has been played out elsewhere, in for instance, Hitler's Germany and Khomeni's Iran. But it follows a familiar and recurrent pattern, and would likely in the United States too. First, the redeemer figure would call for communal integration, urging us to conform to a standard of what a true and obedient American is as part of a solidified and reaffirming tribe. The call for demonic integration leads to the identification of enemies—the different, the critical, the sinful. Because the victim is always guilty, they must be made to suffer. The united community through their redeemer hero calls for victimage. The victim is a scapegoat which the community wills to sacrifice to purge itself of alien elements and collective guilt. Purgation perfects the community. The leader's heroism has thus brought communal redemption through a retributive quest. The salvation of the community is assured.

Yet it is not. If Americans cross the threshold into demonic redemption, it would be difficult to go back to normalcy. A politics of redemption cannot return to ordinary affairs, since the nation and its leader are deluded into believing themselves the agents of a higher purpose. Nor can the society return to ordinary life, which might reintroduce dissident, creative, or vulgar expressions into the culture. Indeed, a politics of redemption would likely suppress much popular culture as we are now used to it. Much of the best of popular culture is irreverent, satirical, and contemptuous of official pomposity. But the logic of redemptive politics is such that popular culture would constitute a threat, so it would be suppressed or even persecuted. For popular culture could easily become one of the enemies of the State that would be identified, punished, and purged. The now "perfected" community could not allow anything so threatening to its integration as free popular expression.

In a future world disorder, wherein the role of the United States has been diminished, such a national quest leading a blood-drenched redemption is possible and not unprecedented. But if something like that comes about we are certainly in a "post-popular" world. Much of what has been described in this book is evidence of the logic of a popular society and its dynamic relationship with politics. A country in the grip of redemptive politics is enacting a very different kind of political logic, one that excludes popular expression from its culture, and demands as a civic duty everyone just saying no to the corrupting lure of forbidden pleasures. There are fundamentalist and neo-conservative intellectuals who provide justification for political controls over what they call "the secular media culture," which, they believe, is propagating "unbelief, materialism, sexual mores and anti-Christian values" antithetical to the "strong majority of 'unsecular America'," polluting the "spiritual environment."[3] With popular culture stigmatized as a seductive and evil force, the new myth of national redemption will expunge it from our purified midst. (In such an Orwellian state, the Popular Culture Association will have to meet in secret.) Watching the American ship of State commanded by a new Ahab, many of us will wonder once again at the fiery quest.

The Immediate Society

There is an alternative popular scenario, one that carries the logic of a popular society to absurd rather than demonic ends. We might call this the American variant of the Huxleyan dystopia, just as the above was the local version of the Orwellian dystopia. The new myth of this world would be speed and not power. Rather than suppressing and persecuting popular culture, that will be one of this brave new world's prime expressions and economic interests. The emphasis will be on play rather than work, expression rather than repression, enjoyment rather than discipline. Rather than establishing stability through an officially-imposed pain, order is perpetuated through an officially-administered pleasure. Such a future would be a society in which popular culture is dominant rather than absent or rendered official. In the "post-popular" society described above, the danger is sensory deprivation resulting in stagnation; in this kind of society, the danger is sensory overload leading to distraction. An Orwellian society would have an unbearable heaviness of being; a Huxleyan society would have an unbearable lightness of being. The former would have a demonic commitment to serious business; the latter would have a farcical commitment to frivolous play.

As American culture develops, we may be seeing the emergence of *the immediate society*. An immediate society is by definition one devoted to the immediate, the now, the convenient and expedient, the sensate and palpable, the self-indulgent and pleasurable. While an Orwellian state focuses attention on the political drama of the State, a Huxleyan society disperses attention to the social drama of the individual. The latter is a culture of narcissism characterized by instant gratification, leisure as the core of life, and consumption as the measure of worth. There is no sense of history, no life-plan, no thought given to the future. All that is important and real is the present, and the pleasures that can be enjoyed in the here and now. People would have no attention span, since what is to be attended to is the fashion at the moment. As Neil Postman remarked, "What Orwell feared were those who would ban books. What Huxley feared was that there would be no reason to ban a book, for there would be no one who wanted to read one...Orwell feared we would become a captive culture. Huxley feared we would become a trivial culture."[4] Our desire for play and focus on the immediate makes us concentrate momentarily on the trivial, those objects of play that distract and amuse us, but also prevent us from taking the larger view.

The immediate society might well be the wave of the future. Alvin Toffler has argued that "from now on the world will be split between the fast and the slow."[5] The pace of life in both work and play would become faster, but not wiser. For an immediate society lacks the ability to use a wide breadth of perspective. History or tradition are ignored or abandoned, since what matters is what's new. But the new is quickly obsolete, like yesterday's newspaper or last month's celebrity. The habit of social memory disappears, and people live in the "fast lane" on the ever-renewed present. For a "throw-away" society abandons products, ideas, and people as quickly as they are considered inexpedient and boring. An immediate society is easily bored, demanding new things in quick succession to fill the moment of now. Cultural objects ranging from Presidents to celebrities, wars to TV shows, ideologies to advertising slogans will quickly become bores when their moment is past. Since such a society is extremely faddish, Andy Warhol's dictum about everyone in the future being famous for fifteen minutes will become all the more relevant. Such a society is driven by the demons of self-indulgence, the desire for vivid experience at the moment. Everyone is motivated by an "I've got to have it now" spirit, determining all to fill their lives with a broad assortment of new things and pursuits. The immediate society carries the logic of consumption to its completion, making for extremities of wastefulness.

In an immediate society, popular culture would play an important, perhaps even central, role. For if it is the primary desire of people to experience things before they are gone, popular culture will elevate entertainment to the center of our future lives. If work diminishes as an ethic and necessity, then time will be filled with play designed for us by popular culture establishments. Futurists tell us that "designed experiences" may take on fantastic proportions. Already those who can afford it amuse themselves in such designed experiences as fantasy baseball camps, dinner theaters in which they become members of the cast, adult fantasies such as spending a day as a circus performer, appearing on a soap opera, going on a Old West cattle drive, or having a harem for a day. Luxury hotel chains and theme parks become increasingly elaborate fantasy playgrounds designed for people to act out their fantasy, be they scuba diving, big game hunting, or driving a race car. Indeed, the Holodeck on the new *Star Trek* is not outside the realm of possibility. Computer scientists are at work on creating "virtual realities," wherein people can actually imagine themselves into other existences and environments, as a lobster at the bottom of the sea, in universes that run backwards, or having sex with a fantasy partner. Soon we will be able to project holograms from our interactive TV sets into our living rooms, acting in plays with holograms. If, say, you have a desire to play the role of Hamlet in Shakespeare's play, you can buy the hologramic play of *Hamlet*, complete except for the role of Hamlet, which you will play in interaction with the other "actors" on your living room stage. Popular culture in such a world will be limited only by the power of our imaginations.

In its mad quest for vivid experiences, an immediate society would further blur the distinction between fantasy and reality. This would accentuate the inability to encompass a wide breadth of perspective, and further focus our attention in living in a perpetual present in which the boundaries of past, present, and future are obscured. Our ability to deal with history and biography, follow traditional narratives, or exercise patience and circumspection in human affairs would be severely diminished. Politics in particular would become highly volatile and transitory, moving quickly across a succession of entertaining moments that soon become a bore to be abandoned. Further, politics as entertaining fare would become more an exercise in fantasy-building than reality-testing, attuned to our dreamiest illusions and anticipating our fantastic expectations. In that eventuality, popular culture as a source of learning has conditioned us to expect a ludenic world of passing pleasures but to deny a painful world of responsibility. In an immediate society, popular culture may teach us to be irresponsible. And indeed, a society based on the immediate experience would be as self-destructive as an Orwellian society of popular repression. For a Huxleyian world would be one of childishness, in which both politics and popular culture encourage us to indulge ourselves as children, making us into immature and spoiled brats. But such a society cannot cope with the harsh realities of the future, such as international political and economic competition. Both our civic and utilitarian roles would atrophy because of our immature incompetence. Unwilling to work, save and invest, delay gratification, and distinguish between illusion and reality, we would become worthless as both citizens and workers. All that would be left is our pursuit of the pleasures of the moment, a quest for satisfaction through expressive individualism run riot.

An Orwellian society would exhibit the popular culture of power, while a Huxleyian society would demonstrate the power of popular culture. As an historical force, popular culture has already had enormous impact on the way we think, feel, and live. In the postmodern future, popular culture could come to be controlled and used by the authorities for their political purposes, essentially transforming popular culture into propaganda. Alternatively, it becomes an instrument of an immediate society engrossed in its own self-indulgence. But popular culture does not have to be either. It could be a force for free expression and civic competence, if it is allowed to flourish in a mature and libertarian society of critical consumers. Popular culture could become a force for political maturity and cultural tolerance, helping to create a future not only of delightful popular expression but also one of civic peace. It depends upon what we learn from the culture of the populace that surrounds and informs our lives.

Notes

Chapter One

[1]Some influential works on culture and popular culture include A.L. Kroeber and Clyde Kluckhohn, *Culture* (New York: Vintage Books, 1963); Bernard Rosenberg and David Manning White (eds.), *Mass Culture: The Popular Arts in America* (New York: The Free Press, 1957); Rosenberg and White (eds.), *Mass Culture Revisited* (New York: Van Nostrand, 1971); David Manning White and John Pendleton (eds.), *Popular Culture: Mirror of American Life* (Regents of the University of California, 1977); more recently, see the collections gathered by the Popular Culture Center at Bowling Green State University, Ohio: Ray B. Browne and Marshall Fishwick (eds.), *Symbiosis: Popular Culture and Other Fields* (Popular, 1988); Browne, Fishwick, and Kevin O. Browne (eds.), *Dominant Symbols in Popular Culture* (Popular, 1990); see also Neil Postman, *Amusing Ourselves to Death: Public Discourse in the Age of Show Business* (New York: Viking Penguin, 1985), and James W. Carey, *Communication as Culture* (Winchester, MA: Unwin Hyman, 1989).

[2]Eric Erickson, *Toys and Reasons: Stages in the Ritualization of Experience* (Norton, 1977): 54.

[3]See the extensive discussion of the popular process in Bruce E. Gronbeck, "Popular Culture, Media, and Political Communication," *New Directions in Political Communication*, eds. David Swanson and Dan Nimmo (Newbury Park: Sage, 1990) 179-216; Clifford Geertz, *The Interpretation of Cultures* (New York: Basic Books, 1973).

[4]Alexis de Tocqueville, *Democracy in America* (many editions).

[5]Bruno Bettleheim, "Letting Children Be Children...While They Can," Chicago *Tribune Magazine* 13 May 1990: 23-25; reprinted from the 1990 *Medical and Health Annual* (Encyclopedia Britannica, 1989).

[6]See the extensive discussion of the American character and aspirations in Robert Bellah, et al., *Habits of the Heart: Individualism and Commitment in American Life* (Berkeley: U of California P, 1985).

[7]Walter R. Fisher, "Reaffirmation and Subversion of the American Dream." *Quarterly Journal of Speech* 59.2 (1973): 160-67.

Chapter Two

[1]Patrick Allitt, "The American Christ," *American Heritage* (November 1988): 128-141.

[2]Jan Harold Brunvand, *The Vanishing Hitchhiker* (New York: Norton, 1981); *The Choking Doberman* (New York: Norton, 1984).

[3]Hadley Cantril, *The Invasion from Mars* (Princeton: Princeton UP, 1940).

179

[4]Michael Calvin McGee, "The 'Ideograph': A Link Between Rhetoric and Ideology." *Quarterly Journal of Speech* 66 (1980): 1-16.

[5]John William Ward, *Andrew Jackson: Symbol for an Age* (New York: Oxford UP, 1955); "The Meaning of Lindbergh's Flight." *American Quarterly* 10 (1958): 3-16.

[6]See James Combs, *Dreaming Heroic Dreams: Ronald Reagan and American Popular Culture* (unpublished manuscript).

[7]Richard Dorson, *American Folklore* (Chicago: U of Chicago P, 1959).

[8]Gary Wills, *Cincinnatus* (Garden City, NY: Doubleday, 1984).

[9]Robert Jewett and John Shelton Lawrence, *The American Monomyth* (Doubleday Anchor, 1977).

[10]See Richard Schickel, *Intimate Strangers: The Culture of Celebrity* (Garden City, NY: Doubleday, 1985).

[11]This was understood clearly in Daniel J. Boorstin's pathbreaking *The Image: A Guide to Pseudo-events in America* (New York: Atheneum, 1973).

[12]Thomas Mann, quoted in Bill Kinser and Neil Kleinman, *The Dream That Was No More a Dream: A Search for Aesthetic Reality in Germany, 1890-1945* (New York: Harper Colophon, 1969) 75.

[13]See my discussion of this in "The Uses of Popular Culture for Political Science," *Symbiosis: Popular Culture and Other Fields*, eds. Ray B. Browne and Marshall W. Fishwick (Bowling Green: Popular, 1988) 59-69.

[14]Donald M. McKale, *Hitler: The Survival Myth* (New York: Stein & Day, 1981).

[15]The idea of world conspiracy is also a theme in literature. See, most recently, Umberto Eco, *Foucault's Pendulum* (New York: Harcourt Brace Jovanovich, 1988).

Chapter Three

[1]Robert Bellah et al., *Habits of the Heart: Individualism and Commitment in American Life* (Berkeley: U of California P, 1985).

[2]Robert Jewett and John Shelton Lawrence, *The American Monomyth* (New York: Doubleday Anchor, 1977).

[3]The literature on the West is vast. The best place to start is the classic Henry Nash Smith, *Virgin Land* (New York: Vintage Books, 1950).

[4]The term is Frederick J. Hacker's, quoted in "Terrorism: Mindless Violence or New International Politics," Chicago *Tribune* 29 Nov. 1979: sec. 2, 3.

[5]John Hellmann, *American Myth and the Legacy of Vietnam* (New York: Columbia UP, 1986).

[6]Janice Hocker Rushing, "The Rhetoric of the American Western Myth." *Communication Monographs* 50 (1983): 14-32.

[7]See Dan Nimmo and James Combs, *Mediated Political Realities*, 2nd ed. (New York: Longman, 1990), chapter 4.

[8]See, for instance, Ray B. Browne, *Heroes and Humanities: Detective Fiction and Culture* (Bowling Green, OH: Popular, 1980).

Chapter Four

[1]Quoted in the "Sports Section" of the Chicago *Tribune*, 10 Nov. 1990: 1.

[2]T.V. Smith and Edward C. Lindeman, *The Democratic Way of Life* (Mentor, 1963).

[3]Martha Wolfenstein, "The Emergence of Fun Morality." *Journal of Social Issues* 7 (1951): 10-15.

[4]"The Golfing Society," Chicago *Tribune* Sports Section 2, Aug. 1990: 2.

[5]See Heartley W. "Hunk" Anderson with Emil Klosinski, *Notre Dame, Chicago Bears, and Hunk: Football Memoirs in Highlight* (Oviedo, FL: Florida Sun-Gator Publishing Co., 1976).

[6]The classic argument for this is, of course, Johan Huizilnga, *Homo Ludens* (Boston: Beacon, 1956).

[7]See my treatment of "Field of Dreams" in *American Political Movies* (New York: Garland, 1990).

[8]Louis Kaufman et al., *Moe Berg: Athlete, Scholar...Spy* (Ballantine, 1976).

Chapter Five

[1]This is an argument made by such varied observers as Alexis de Tocqueville and William James; a theoretical discussion of the reasons for the atrophy or diffusion of belief is Michael and Deena Weinstein. "Simmel and the Dialectic of the Double Boundary: The Case of the Metropolis and Mental Life." *Social Inquiry* 59.1 (1989): 48-59.

[2]Patrick Allitt, "The American Christ." *American Heritage* (1988): 128-141.

[3]Frances Fitzgerald, "Jim and Tammy," *The New Yorker* 23 Apr. 1990: 45-48, 50, 67-87.

[4]Richard Neuhaus, *The Naked Public Square* (Grand Rapids, MI: W.B. Eerdmans, 1984).

[5]See Joseph Gusfield, *Symbolic Crusade* (Urbana: U of Illinios P, 1966).

[6]Gary Wills, "The Phallic Pulpit," *New York Review of Books* 21 Dec. 1989: 19-26.

[7]Gary Wills, "The Private Ministry of Colonel Thieme (Marilyn Quayle's Theologian)." *Wigwag* 1 (1989): 3-23.

[8]See Pat Robertston and Bob Slosser, *The Secret Kingdom* (Nashville, TN: Thomas Nelson, 1982).

[9]Robert W. Faid, *Gorbachev: Has the Real Antichrist Come?* (Tulsa, OK: Victory House, 1989).

[10]Margaret Atwood, *The Handmaid's Tale* (New York: Houghton Mifflin, 1986).

[11]Lewis Lapham, *Money and Class in America: Notes and Observations on Our Civil Religion* (New York: Weidenfeld & Nicolson, 1988).

[12]J. Hoberman and Jonathan Rosenbaum, "The Idolmakers." *American Film* (Dec. 1982): 48-55.

Part II

[1]David Thornburn, "Television as as Aesthetic Medium." *Critical Studies in Mass Communication* 4 (1987): 166.

[2]John Cawelti, "With the Benefit of Hindsight: Popular Culture Criticism." *Critical Studies in Mass Communication* 2 (1985): 369.

[3]Thomas M. Lessl, "The Priestly Voice." *Quarterly Journal of Speech* 75 (1989): 183-197.

Chapter Six

[1]David L. Althiede and Robert P. Snow, *Media Logic* (Beverly Hills, CA: Sage, 1979).

[2]William Stephenson, *The Play Theory of Mass Communication* (Chicago: U of Chicago P, 1967).

[3]Daniel Boorstin, *The Image* (New York: Atheneum, 1973).

[4]John L. Caughey, "Artificial Social Relations in Modern America." *American Quarterly* 30:1 (1978): 70-89.

[5]John Cawelti, *Adventure, Mystery, Romance* (Chicago: U of Chicago P, 1976).

[6]"Are Kids Growing Up Too Fast?" *Redbook* (March 1990): 91-100.

[7]Stanley J. Baran et al, "You Are What You Buy: Mass-Mediated Judgements of People's Worth." *Journal of Communication* 39.2: 46-54.

[8]*Redbook* report, op. cit.: 95.

[9]Lary May, *Screening Out the Past: The Birth of Mass Culture and the Motion Picture Industry* (New York: Oxford UP, 1980).

[10]George Gerbner and L.P. Gross, "The Scary World of TV's Heavy Viewer." *Psychology Today* (April 1976): 41ff.

[11]Bruce Gronbeck, "Popular Culture, Media, and Political Communication," *New Directions in Political Communication*, eds. David Swanson and Dan Nimmo (Newbury Park: Sage, 1990) 205; for various views of those multiple meanings, see *Politics in Familiar Contexts*, eds. Robert Savage and Dan Nimmo (Ablex, 1990).

[12]Mark Crispin Miller, "Big Brother is You Watching." *Georgia Review* 38 (1984): 695-719.

[13]John Fiske, *Television Culture* (London: Metheun, 1987).

Chapter Seven

[1]See James Combs and Dan Nimmo, *The New Propaganda: The Dictatorship of Palaver in Contemporary Politics* (White Plains, NY: Longman, 1992).

[2]See, for instance, Grant McCracken, *Culture and Consumption* (Bloomington, IN: Indiana UP, 1988).

[3]Jacques Ellul, *Propaganda: The Formation of Men's Attitudes* (New York: Random House, 1965).

[4]See Phillip Kotler, " 'Dream' Vacations: The Booming Market for Designed Experiences." *Futurist* 18 (October 1984): 7-13.

[5]"Profile of an Army," Chicago *Tribune* 20 Dec. 1990: 2.

[6]See Maureen Honey, *Creating Rosie the Riveter: Class, Gender, and Propaganda During World War II* (U of Massachusetts, 1984); Carol Moog, *Are They Selling Her Lips? Advertising and Identity* (William Morrow, 1990).

[7]Thomas R. Dye and L. Harmon Zeigler, *The Irony of Democracy* (Tuxbury, 1984).

[8]James W. Gibson, *The Perfect War* (Boston: Atlantic Monthly, 1986).

[9]Richard Gid Powers, *G-Men: Hoover's FBI in American Popular Culture* (Carbondale, IL.: Southern Illinios UP, 1983).

Chapter Eight

[1]John Shelton Lawrence. " 'Entertainment': The Ritual Center of American Culture." (Unpublished paper: Morningside College, Iowa).

[2]Richard Schickel, *D.W. Griffith: An American Life* (New York: Simon & Schuster, 1984) 467.

[3]For a wide-ranging view of celebrity, see *Celebrity*, ed. James Monaco (New York: Dell, 1978).

[4]Daniel Dayan and Elihu Katz, "Television Ceremonial Events." *Society* 22 (1985): 60-66.

[5]Mark de la Vina, "Future Shock: Salaries But No Work," Chicago *Tribune* 12 Jan. 1991: sec. 2, 3.

[6]Harry Frankfurt, "On Bullshit." *Raritan* 6 (1986): 81-100.

[7]See the formulation of this idea in Jean Baudrillard, *Simulations* (New York: Semiotext, 1983); and James Combs, "Towards 2084: Continuing the Orwellian Tradition," *The Orwellian Moment: Hindsight and Foresight in the Post-1984 World*, eds. Robert Savage et al. (Fayetteville: U of Arkansas P, 1989).

[8]Donald Kanter and Phillip Mirvis, *The Cynical Americans* (Jossey-Bass, 1989).

Chapter Nine

[1]But see the brilliant essays by Chilean author Ariel Dorfman, *How to Read Donald Duck* (London: International General, 1975), and *The Empire's Old Clothes* (New York: Pantheon, 1983); and Roger Rollin, *The Americanization of the Global Village* (Bowling Green, OH: Popular, 1990).

[2]Ernest Callenbach, *Ecotopia* (Banyan Tree, 1975; Bantam, 1983 and 1990).

[3]Robert Heilbroner, *An Inquiry into the Human Prospect* (New York: Norton, 1980) 172-73.

[4]Bernard Crick, *George Orwell* (Boston: Little, Brown, 1980).

[5]Margaret Atwood, *The Handmaid's Tale* (New York: Houghton Mifflin, 1986).

Conclusion

[1]Robert Jewett and John Shelton Lawrence, *The American Monomyth* (Doubleday Anchor, 1977).

[2]James Combs and Dan Nimmo, *Subliminal Politics* (Englewood Cliffs, NJ: Prentice-Hall, 1980) 240-243.

[3]See the recent arguments of Michael Novak, including "American Catholics: Diverse Groups in One Nation," Chicago *Tribune* 24 Mar. 1989: 15.

[4]Neil Postman, *Amusing Ourselves to Death* (New York: Penguin Books, 1986) vii.

[5]Alvin Toffler, "Toffler's Next Shock." *World Monitor* (November, 1990): 34.